Basics of
Mortgage-Backed
Securities

Joseph Hu, Ph.D.

Published by Frank J. Fabozzi Associates

© 1997 By Frank J. Fabozzi Associates
New Hope, Pennsylvania

This publication is designed to provide accurate and authoritative information in regard to the subject matter covered. It is sold with the understanding that the publisher is not engaged in rendering legal, accounting, or other professional services.

The views expressed in this book are solely those of the author, not necessarily those of the author's employer, Oppenheimer & Co., Inc.

ISBN: 1-883249-21-X

Printed in the United States of America

*To
Linda,
Justin and Brian*

About the Author

Dr. Joseph C. Hu is Managing Director and Director of Mortgage Research at Oppenheimer & Co., Inc. Prior to joining Oppenheimer, he was Senior Vice President and Head of Mortgage Research at Nomura Securities International, Inc., Executive Vice President and Director of Mortgage Research at Shearson Lehman Hutton Inc., Senior Vice President and Head of Mortgage Research and Strategy Group at E.F. Hutton Inc., Vice President at Salomon Brothers Inc., and Economist at Federal National Mortgage Association. He also served as Associate Planner at Oklahoma City Planning Department and as Assistant Professor in Economics Department of the University of Maine.

Dr. Hu received his Ph.D. in economics from Oklahoma State University in 1974; M.A. degree from the University of New Mexico in 1971; and B.A. degree from the National Taiwan University in 1968.

Table of Contents

Preface

The purpose of *Basics of Mortgage-Backed Securities* is to provide readers with a basic but comprehensive understanding of this investment instrument. It is intended for fixed income portfolio managers who would like to diversify and enhance their performance through mortgage-backed securities (MBSs). Despite the fact that the MBS sector represents 30% of the domestic taxable fixed income market, many managers learn about these securities piecemeal on the job. They may lack a comprehensive view of MBSs, a view that is critical to be an effective manager. This book is also useful for business students at both the undergraduate and graduate levels.

Basics of Mortgage-Backed Securities is essentially a synopsis of over 100 articles and special reports on various subjects pertaining to MBSs that I have authored over the past 15 years. The book begins with an introduction and description of different types of residential mortgages and the participants in the primary residential mortgage market. It then chronologically presents the evolution of MBSs from a single class format to a variety of multiple maturity classes. It also provides a brief history of federal agencies as guarantors of MBSs. Mortgage prepayment is discussed extensively to equip readers with a fundamental appreciation of the uniqueness of MBSs. A chapter on basic mortgage math is presented to demonstrate quantitatively how MBSs differ from other fixed income securities. Finally, to apply the basic product knowledge to making profitable investments, this book devotes the last three chapters to the analysis of relative value and performance of MBSs.

This book would not have been possible without the generous support of the management of Oppenheimer & Co., Inc., in particular, Thomas Gallagher, Vice Chairman. I am grateful of the collegial help and encouragement from Alan Leiderman, Oppenheimer's Director of Mortgage Securities Trading and Sales, who reviewed and commented on all chapters. Benjamin Stone, Edward Brown, Michael Julius, and William Malone, respectively, traders of fixed-rate, adjustable-rate pass-throughs, agency-guaranteed, and private-label REMICs, reviewed the chapters relating to their specific expertise. Ian Jaffe, mortgage research analyst, proofread an early draft of the book.

I would also like to thank those who contributed to the preparation of *Basics of Mortgage-Backed Securities*. Specifically, Charles Clark of Ginnie Mae, Gene Spencer and Wayne McLurkin of Fannie Mae, and Sharon McHale and Douglas Robinson of Freddie Mac assisted in describing the specifics and the histories of their respective agency-guaranteed MBS programs. Craig Cohen of Piper Jaffray, Howard Esaki of Morgan Stanley, and David Chow of Fortis Asset Management provided valuable comments on selected chapters. I, of course, am responsible for the inevitable omissions and possible errors in the book.

Joseph Hu
January 1997

Chapter 1

Residential Mortgages

- Definition of a Single-Family Mortgage
- Features of a Fixed-Rate Mortgage
- Alternatives to 30-Year FRMs

DEFINITION OF A SINGLE-FAMILY MORTGAGE

A *mortgage* is a loan secured by the pledge of a specific piece of real estate property. Strictly speaking, the term "mortgage" refers only to the pledge of property given by the *mortgagor* (the borrower) to the *mortgagee* (the lender), not the promissory note that it secures. In general use, however, the term refers to both. The legal characterization of a mortgage differs among states in terms of "title" and "lien." In the so-called "title states," a mortgage represents the actual transfer of the title from the mortgagor to the mortgagee. The mortgage is canceled by repayment of the debt. In the "lien states," a mortgage simply grants the mortgagee a lien on the property that secures the mortgage.

The broad class of mortgages includes residential and non-residential mortgages. A residential mortgage can be secured by a single-family, two- to four-family, or multi-family property. A non-residential mortgage is secured by either a commercial building or a farm property. Throughout this book, unless otherwise specified, the term residential mortgage refers to a single-family mortgage.

A single-family mortgage consists of many lengthy documents. In essence, it sets forth the amount of the loan, the obligation of the mortgagor to repay the loan, a description of the pledged property (a single-family house), and the mortgagor's ownership interest in the property. It also contains specifications as to the maintenance and insurance of the property and the payment of taxes and any prior mortgages. The promissory note delineates the annual interest rate, the amortization period, the final maturity, and the monthly payment amount for the mortgage loan.

FEATURES OF A FIXED-RATE MORTGAGE

The basic features of a fixed-rate mortgage are: the amortization period, the stated interest rate, the frequency of mortgage payments, and in certain cases, the type of insurance against possible default. Prior to the 1980s, mortgages almost always carried a fixed interest rate with a 30-year amortization period and a constant (level) monthly payment. They are referred to as *level-payment, fixed-rate mortgages* (FRMs).

A FRM is repaid by a constant monthly payment throughout its maturity term. The monthly payment consists of repayment of principal and interest on the remaining principal. The gradual paydown of a mortgage is called *amortization*. Given the size of the original balance of the mortgage, the monthly payment varies according to the mortgage rate. The composition of the monthly payment in principal and interest also varies with different mortgage rates. Exhibits 1 to 4 demonstrate the amortization of two 30-year FRMs. One FRM carries a 5% interest rate; the other, 20%. Both have an original loan amount of $100,000. (The algebraic derivation of the monthly payment will be presented in Chapter 5.) Several observations can be generalized:

1. The higher the mortgage rate, the higher will be the monthly payment. The 5% mortgage has a monthly payment of $537, whereas that of the 20% mortgage is $1,671 (Exhibits 1 and 2).
2. While the monthly payment remains unchanged for the term of a FRM, its composition of principal and interest changes monthly.
3. In the early years of a FRM, the monthly payment is represented mainly by the interest payment. The repayment of principal is only a minor portion of the early monthly payment. As the mortgage ages, however, the importance of principal repayment increases and the significance of interest payment decreases correspondingly.

Exhibit 1: Amortization of a 5% Mortgage: Monthly Principal and Interest Payment per $100,000 Original Principal

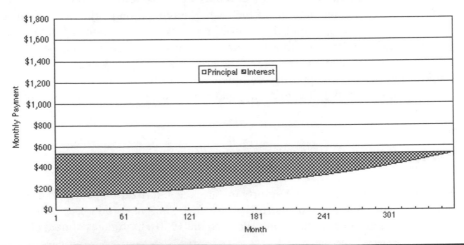

Exhibit 2: Amortization of a 20% Mortgage: Monthly Principal and Interest Payment per $100,000 Original Principal

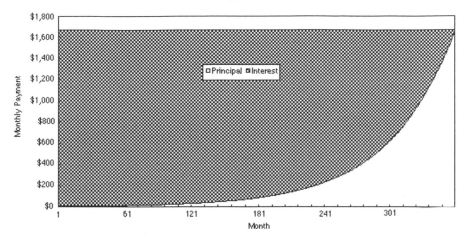

Exhibit 3: Amortization of a 5% Mortgage: Monthly Remaining Balance per $100,000 Original Principal

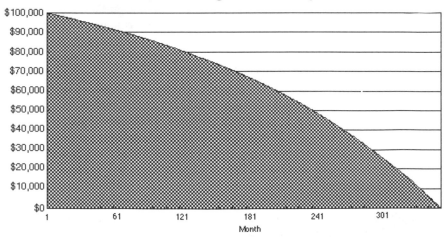

4. A mortgage carrying a lower interest rate amortizes faster than the one carrying a higher rate. As Exhibit 3 shows, close to $20,000 of the $100,000 original principal of the 5% mortgage is already repaid by the beginning of the 10th year. By contrast, Exhibit 4 shows that, by the 10th year, less than $2,000 of the principal is repaid for the 20% mortgage.

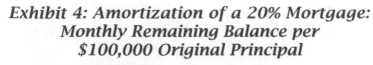

Exhibit 4: Amortization of a 20% Mortgage: Monthly Remaining Balance per $100,000 Original Principal

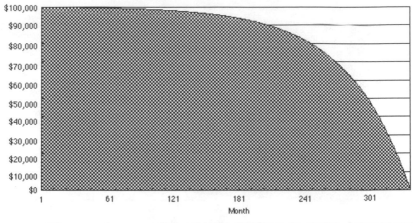

ALTERNATIVES TO 30-YEAR FRMS

Since the 1970s, 30-year FRMs have been the predominant instrument of housing finance in the mortgage market. However, other types of mortgages have from time to time served as alternatives to FRMs. Depending on the market environment and levels of interest rates, these alternative mortgages are attractive to either lenders or home buyers for various reasons.

Adjustable-Rate Mortgages (ARMs)

In the early 1980s, when inflation was rampant and mortgage rates were high and volatile, ARMs became popular for both home buyers and mortgage lenders. The inflationary environment made it difficult for lenders to offer 30-year FRMs. Rising interest rates caused an asset-liability maturity mismatch for banks and thrifts (then the major mortgage lenders), which had been financing long-term mortgages primarily with short-term deposits. These lenders desired assets with shorter maturities. Furthermore, high interest rates raised monthly payments substantially, making it difficult for home buyers to qualify for FRMs. (As a general rule for mortgage underwriting, home buyers need to have an annual after-tax income at least three times the annual mortgage payment in order to qualify for a mortgage loan.) These problems made ARMs attractive alternatives to 30-year FRMs.

In general, an ARM still has a 30-year amortization period, but its interest rate is adjustable — mostly on an annual basis. (A detailed discussion of ARMs and ARM pass-throughs is presented in Chapter 6.) The interest rate adjustment (the "rate reset") is based on an index rate plus a spread (called "margin," usually 150 to 300 basis points). The index rate can be a series of money-market interest rates, such as interest rates on three-, six-, or 12-month Treasury bills. It can also be a cost of funds index, based on the interest cost of liabilities to thrifts.

Although the interest rate on an ARM is adjustable, it is not without limitation. A great majority of ARMs have "caps" for both the periodical reset (periodical cap) and lifetime reset (lifetime cap). ARMs are attractive to borrowers primarily because they are offered at an initial rate that is well below the prevailing FRM rate. Therefore, they have lower initial payments, though not necessarily lower lifetime payments.

Fifteen-Year Fixed-Rate Mortgages

Another response to the high interest rate prevalent in the 1980s was the 15-year FRM. Like a 30-year FRM, a 15-year mortgage continues to have a fixed interest rate, but its amortization period is only half of that of a 30-year FRM. Due to the shorter amortization period, the monthly payment of a 15-year mortgage is represented far more significantly by the repayment of principal than a 30-year mortgage. This is particularly true in the early years. The faster repayment of principal and the shorter overall maturity make 15-year mortgages attractive to lenders. For these reasons, 15-year mortgages are offered at lower rates than 30-year mortgages. Additionally, 15-year mortgages were made more attractive by the 1986 Tax Reform Act, which lowered marginal tax rates. With lower marginal tax rates, the deductibility of the mortgage interest payment for income tax purposes became less valuable to homeowners. This reduced the tax advantage of the slower amortizing 30-year mortgages and favored 15-year mortgages.

Graduated-Payment Mortgages (GPMs)

Other less popular mortgages were also offered in the 1980s to address the issue of home affordability caused by high mortgage rates. A GPM has a 30-year maturity, but a markedly lower monthly payment in the first year than a comparable rate level-payment FRM. The first year's low payment rises gradually for a predetermined period and then levels off. Because of the low initial payment, a GPM has "negative amortization" in the early years. That is, the remaining principal balance of the mortgage rises (negatively amortizes) initially rather than declines at the outset as in the case of a level-payment FRM.

Growing Equity Mortgages (GEMs)

Like a GPM, a GEM also has a low initial monthly payment that increases gradually, but no negative amortization. The rising monthly payment of a GEM is designed to build up the equity for the home owner through a faster amortization schedule (thus the name "growing equity"). Because of the quicker amortization, the final maturity of a GEM is significantly shorter than 30 years, although the initial payment is figured on a 30-year schedule. The shorter final maturity allows the lender to charge a lower rate on the mortgage, therefore lowering the initial monthly payment of a GEM.

Biweekly Mortgages

Based on the same concept of building up equity more quickly while maintaining a level payment, a biweekly mortgage was developed. Since increasingly paychecks have been distributed on a biweekly basis, it would be convenient for mortgagors to write checks for the mortgage payment on payday. More important, a biweekly mortgage entails 26 payments (or "13" monthly payments) a year. It accelerates the amortization of the mortgage and shortens its final maturity to less than 30 years. Because of its shorter maturity, a biweekly mortgage is offered at a slightly lower rate than a 30-year mortgage.

Balloon Mortgages

Balloon mortgages also have a 30-year amortization schedule, but are due in just five or seven years (thus the name "balloon"). Balloons are suitable for homeowners who have a tendency to move frequently. Since they do not plan to stay at a residence for a long period of time, they do not need to obtain 30-year financing for home purchases. However, they do need the financing which amortizes on a 30-year schedule. For them, balloons are ideal mortgages. Again, the shorter final maturity of balloon mortgages entails lower mortgage rates. It reduces the monthly payment and makes balloons popular among homeowners who are "frequent movers."

In general, among the variety of alternatives to 30-year FRMs, ARMs have proved the most popular. Over the past decade, a differing mix of fixed- and adjustable-rate mortgages has been originated, depending on the interest rate environment. When interest rates were high, such as in 1984 and 1988, ARMs were popular among home buyers, and more ARMs than traditional FRMs were originated. By contrast, in 1992-93, when long-term rate were at historically low levels, FRMs accounted for nearly 80% of all mortgage originations. More recently, ARMs have accounted for approximately 30% of total originations. Fifteen-year FRMs have proved less popular, except during the refinancing boom of 1992-93, when many homeowners took advantage of low rates to refinance 30-year loans at roughly the same payments but shorter maturities.

Chapter 2

The U.S. Residential Mortgage Market

- The Origination of a Mortgage
- Major Mortgage Lenders
- Mortgage Servicers
- Mortgage Insurers
- The Size of the Primary Mortgage Market

THE ORIGINATION OF A MORTGAGE

The mortgage origination process begins with a prospective home buyer (the borrower) applying for a mortgage loan from an originator (the lender). For most Americans, obtaining a mortgage is one of their most important — and often the largest — financial transactions. A lender will consider four things before making a mortgage loan: the borrower's current income in relation to the size of the mortgage loan, the borrower's credit history, the appraised value of the house that secures the mortgage, and the size of down payment for the loan.

Debt-to-Income Ratio
The lender considers the current income of the borrower in relation to the expense of owning the house that secures the loan. The bulk of the expense is the so-called *P.I.T.I.*: monthly payment of *principal* and *interest* of the mortgage, the property *tax*, and the homeowner's *insurance* (property insurance and mortgage insurance, if applicable). As a rule of thumb, the *debt-to-income ratio* — the ratio of P.I.T.I. to monthly income — should not exceed 25% to 28%. Additionally, the lender reviews the long- and short-term liabilities of the borrower. A borrower who is heavily in debt would need a lower income-to-expense ratio in order to qualify for the mortgage loan.

Credit History
The credit history of the borrower is important because it reflects the way the borrower handles financial responsibilities. Most often the credit history includes the payment history of various credit cards and other types of short-term loans. A borrower with an excellent credit history has accounts that are always "current." By contrast, frequent lapses of payments for these accounts suggest a bad credit history. Although these lapses are sometimes unavoidable due to unexpected

events such as unemployment, illness, or other financial strains, they do serve as a warning for the lender regarding the financial conditions of the borrower. Currently, credit reports of borrowers often rank them by a scoring system into A, B, C, and D categories. Category A borrowers have the lowest credit risk, and Category D the highest risk.

Property Appraisal

Since a mortgage is secured by a house, the appraised market value of the house figures importantly in the lender's decision of whether or not to make a mortgage loan. Thus, as a part of the application for a mortgage loan, the borrower has to supply the lender with the market value of the house as appraised by a professional and certified property appraiser. The appraised value has to be no less than the purchase price of the house.

Down Payment

Typically, a lender will finance only 80% to 90% of the purchase price of a house. The remaining 10% to 20% is paid directly as down payment by the borrower. The ratio of loan amount to the purchase price of the house is called the *loan-to-value ratio* (LTV). For example, a home buyer purchases a house that is worth $100,000 but pays out of pocket only $20,000 as down payment. The rest of the purchase price is financed by a lender through a mortgage loan. The LTV for the loan is 80%. As will be discussed in a later section, a mortgage loan with an LTV exceeding 80% generally requires "mortgage insurance." For low- and moderate-income home buyers who cannot afford a sizable down payment, loans with LTVs in the high 90s have been originated. These loans are generally insured by government agencies.

MAJOR MORTGAGE LENDERS

Residential mortgages have been traditionally originated by three major lenders: commercial banks, thrifts, and mortgage bankers. Commercial banks and thrifts are depository lenders. They traditionally have funded mortgage originations with deposits, although this type of funding has become increasingly unimportant. Mortgage bankers are non-depository lenders. They fund originations with short-term lines of credit from commercial banks. They repay the short-term financing by selling their newly originated mortgages in the "secondary" mortgage market. (The marketplace where lenders deal with borrowers is the "primary" mortgage market. The secondary mortgage market is where lenders deal with investors.) Combined, these three lenders have always accounted for more than 90% of annual total originations. More impressive, as shown in Exhibit 1, in recent years, their combined market share has grown to virtually 100%. Among them, mortgage bankers have increasingly become the most important lender, responsible for about 50% of total originations. This expansion was at the expense of both commercial banks and thrifts.

Exhibit 1: Market Share of Residential Mortgage Originations, Major Lenders, 1970-1995

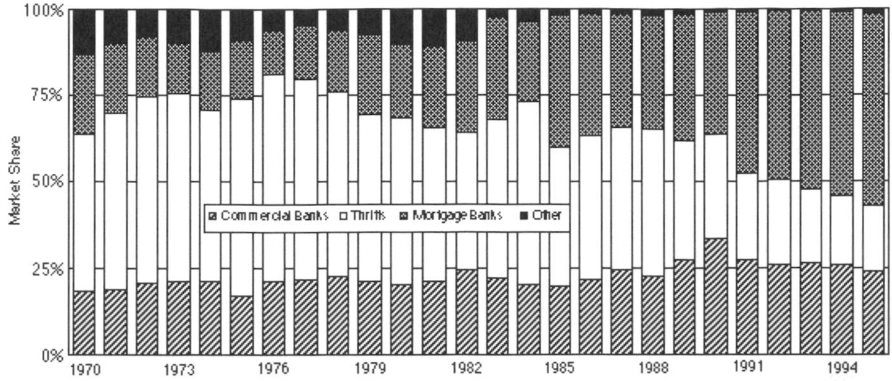

Source: U.S. Department of Housing and Urban Development

Mortgage lenders earn a fee for originating mortgages. This origination fee is expressed in "points," where one point equals one percent of the mortgage loan balance. In recent years, the origination fee has averaged just under two points. After mortgages are originated, depository lenders can choose either to hold these mortgages in their own portfolios as investments or sell them to investors. Non-depository lenders, however, must always sell their newly originated loans to investors.

MORTGAGE SERVICERS

When newly originated mortgages are sold in the secondary market or held in the portfolios of their originators, they have to be "serviced." This servicing function entails collecting monthly payments from the mortgagors and forwarding them to the investors, sending payment and overdue notices to the mortgagors, maintaining principal balance records, administering escrow accounts (prepaid balances by mortgagors) for real estate taxes and insurance premiums, advancing payments to investors on behalf of mortgagors in case of delinquencies and defaults, and initiating foreclosure and maintaining the underlying houses when mortgages are in default.

Servicers include bank- or thrift-related entities and mortgage bankers. Mortgage originators can either maintain the servicing responsibility and fees, or sell them to other servicers. The servicers earn revenue from a number of sources, including the servicing fee (a fixed percentage of the outstanding mortgage balance, typically 30 to 45 basis points), the interest earned on escrow accounts, the float earned on the delay between the receipt and the forwarding of mortgage payments to the owners of mortgages, and fees charged on late payments.

MORTGAGE INSURERS

Single-family mortgages are debt instruments. Like all private debts, they entail credit risk. For various social, economic, and demographic reasons such as divorce, unemployment, or unexpected financial strains, borrowers may fail to continue to make their monthly payments. A mortgage is generally considered in default if the borrower fails to make the monthly payment in three consecutive months.

Historically, the incidence of mortgage default is positively associated with the mortgage's original LTV ratio. The risk of mortgage default is particularly high when the LTV exceeds 80%. For that reason, to originate a mortgage that has a LTV exceeding 80%, the lender often requires that the mortgage be insured.

Mortgage insurance can be provided either by a federal government agency or a private mortgage insurance company (MIC). The Federal Housing Administration (FHA) provides mortgage insurance mainly to promote home ownership for low- and moderate-income families. The Department of Veterans Affairs (VA) guarantees mortgages as a benefit for veterans. MICs, however, provide mortgage insurance for profit as a private enterprise.

FHA Insurance

The FHA was created under the National Housing Act of 1934. The insurance coverage by FHA is for the entire loan amount, although the amount is subject to an administrative limit. Due to a wide range of housing prices among regions, the FHA limit varies depending on the location of the property. The standard FHA insurance limit is $67,500. For high cost areas, the limit can be as high as $155,250. There is an insurance premium charged by FHA and paid by the borrower. In case of default, the FHA has two options: (1) pay the lender the insured amount and let the lender take the title of the house or (2) reimburse the lender for the entire loan amount and take the title of the house itself.

VA Guarantee

The Servicemen's Readjustment Act of 1944 authorized the VA to guarantee mortgage loans made to eligible veterans. Unlike FHA insurance, the VA guarantee is for only a fraction of the loan amount. It is limited to $36,000 if the loan amount is less than $144,000. The maximum coverage could increase to $50,750 or 25% of the loan amount, whichever is less, if the loan exceeds $144,000. Unlike FHA-guaranteed loans, there is no premium charged for a VA-insured loan. Like FHA, however, the VA provides two types of recourse in case of default: (1) the lender takes the title and forfeits the VA guarantee, or (2) the VA pays the guaranteed amount, but takes the title of the house.

RHS Guarantee

To a limited extent, mortgage loans secured by single-family houses on farm properties are guaranteed by the Rural Housing Service (RHS). This agency replaced the former Farmers Home Administration (FmHA).

Exhibit 2: Mortgage Insurance Companies by Credit Ratings, Net New Issuance, and Market Share, 1995

Mortgage Insurance Company	Credit Rating	Issuance ($ Billion)	Market Share (%)
Amerin Guaranty Co.	Not Rated	5.86	5.3
Commonwealth Mortgage Assurance Co.	AA	10.59	9.6
General Electric Mortgage Insurance Co.	AAA	22.06	20.1
Mortgage Guaranty Insurance Co.*	AA–	30.18	27.4
PMI Mortgage Insurance Co.	AA	14.79	13.5
Republic Mortgage Insurance Co.	AA–	10.65	9.7
Triad Guaranty Insurance Co.	AA	1.61	1.5
United Guaranty Residential Insurance Co.	AAA	14.13	12.9
Total		109.87	100

* Includes CMG mortgage Insurance Co.

Source: Duff & Phelps Credit Rating Co. and *The Mortgage Market Statistical Annual for 1996*, reprinted with permission of Inside Mortgage Finance Publications, Inc., Bethesda, Maryland. (310-951-1240)

Private Mortgage Insurance

Mortgages that are not insured by government agencies are called "conventional" mortgages. Depending on their LTVs, these mortgages can be either insured by a MIC or not insured at all. Currently, there are eight major providers of private mortgage insurance. (See Exhibit 2.) These eight MICs are the bulk of the private mortgage insurance industry. This industry has existed since the 1920s. However, poor underwriting and lack of adequate reserves to meet emergencies led to the industry's collapse in the early 1930s. After reappearing in the mid-1950s, the private mortgage insurance industry has existed without any financial failure. The number of MICs, however, has changed from time to time.

As shown in Exhibit 2, the credit rating of the eight MICs ranges from AA– to AAA. Regulated by state laws and restricted by statutes to operate as single-line companies, MICs can write credit insurance only on residential mortgages. Most privately insured mortgages have LTVs of 90% to 95%. MICs generally insure 25% of the face amount of 90% LTV loans and 25%-30% of 95% LTV loans. If an insured conventional mortgage goes into default, a MIC has two options to fulfill its insurance obligation. First, it can pay up to the specified mortgage insurance coverage to the lender and let the lender retain the property for liquidation. Second, a MIC can reimburse the lender for the entire loan amount and take title to the property for liquidation. Any expenses associated with selling the property will be absorbed by the MIC.

THE SIZE OF THE PRIMARY MORTGAGE MARKET

Over the past two decades, originations of single-family mortgages have grown rapidly. As shown in Exhibit 3, by the mid-1970s, annual originations were already around $100 billion. (The terms of single-family and one- to four-family have often been used interchangeably because an overwhelming majority of originations are single-family mortgages.) By 1993, when mortgage rates plunged to their lowest levels in 25 years, originations exceeded $1 trillion. Brisk housing activity sustained by baby boomers has been the major force contributing to the persistently voluminous originations. Refinancing, which was particularly active in 1986-87 and 1991-93, was another important factor. In 1994-95, however, originations fell to $780 and $650 billion, respectively. They were caused primarily by diminished refinancing due to rising mortgage rates.

Despite huge annual originations, the net increase in mortgage debt — a balance obtained by netting out mortgage prepayments from originations — has been far smaller than originations (also Exhibit 3). In particular, the net increase in mortgage debt in 1992-93 amounted to only a fraction of originations. Historically low mortgage rates have always triggered strong waves of refinancing. Since refinancing basically replaces old mortgages with the same amount of new mortgages, it results in voluminous originations but little net increase in mortgage debt.

Measured in terms of outstanding balance, the residential mortgage market is the largest single sector of the U.S. capital markets. As of year end 1995, outstanding residential mortgages amounted to just over $4 trillion (Exhibit 4). About 90% of this amount were single-family mortgages; the remaining 10%, multifamily mortgages. Of the $3.7 trillion single-family mortgages, nearly 45% have been pooled for the issuance of mortgage pass-through securities, the subject of the next chapter (Exhibit 5).

Exhibit 3: Annual Originations of One- to Four-Family Mortgages and Net Increase in Mortgage Debt
1970 to 1996*

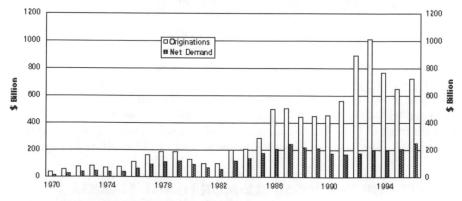

* Figures for 1996 are annualized based on six-month data.
Sources: U.S. Department of Housing and Urban Development and *Flow of Funds Accounts*, Board of Governors of the Federal Reserve System

Exhibit 4: Size of Capital Markets, Outstanding Non-Financial Debt by Issuer, as of Second Quarter 1996

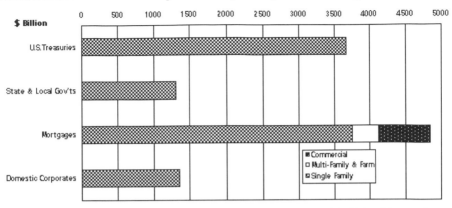

Source: *Flow of Funds Accounts of the United States*, Board of Governors of the Federal Reserve System

Exhibit 5: Outstanding Mortgage Debt by Type, as of Second Quarter 1996

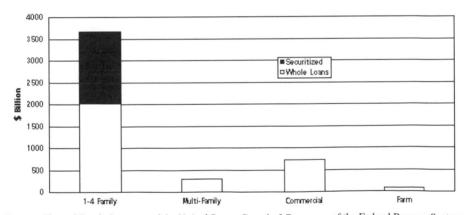

Source: *Flow of Funds Accounts of the United States*, Board of Governors of the Federal Reserve System

Chapter 3

Mortgage Pass-Through Securities

- Definition of Mortgage Pass-Through Securities
- Ginnie Mae Mortgage Pass-Throughs
- Freddie Mac Participation Certificates
- Fannie Mae Mortgage-Backed Securities
- Private-Label Pass-Throughs
- Current Trading of Pass-Throughs

DEFINITION OF MORTGAGE PASS-THROUGH SECURITIES

A *mortgage pass-through security*, or simply a mortgage pass-through, is backed by a pool of mortgages whose monthly payments are the sole source of cash flow of the security. The security is called a "pass-through" because monthly payments generated from the underlying pool of mortgages are "passed" from mortgagors "through" the issuer to investors in the security. Since pass-throughs are backed by pools of mortgages, they are generically called *mortgage-backed securities*.

By issuing a mortgage pass-through, the issuer is in fact selling the direct ownership interest in the underlying pool of mortgages to investors. By purchasing mortgage pass-throughs, investors are indirect but ultimate providers of mortgage funds to home buyers. Thus, the issuance of mortgage pass-throughs channels credit from the capital markets to the housing market. Over the past 20 years, when housing demand has been historically strong, mortgage pass-throughs have been critically important in financing brisk housing activity and achieving high levels of home ownership.

GINNIE MAE MORTGAGE PASS-THROUGHS

Mortgage pass-throughs were first issued by mortgage bankers in 1970. They issued mortgage securities backed by newly originated FHA, VA, and, to a limited degree, RHS mortgages (formerly FmHA-insured mortgages). In addition to the cash flows of their underlying mortgages, which are already insured or guaranteed by agencies of the federal government, the credit of the pass-throughs is further enhanced by the guarantee of the *Government National Mortgage Association*, commonly known as *Ginnie Mae*. (For convenience, it will be referred to as GNMA throughout the book.) GNMA is a wholly owned U.S. government corporation created by Congress under the Housing and Urban Development Act of 1968, which also established the Department of Housing and Urban Development (HUD). GNMA is a part of HUD. The pass-throughs guaranteed by GNMA are often referred to as Ginnie Maes (hereafter, GNMAs).

During the first half of the 1970s, issuance of GNMAs was quite modest by modern standards: it never surpassed $10 billion per year (Exhibit 1). However, issuance of GNMAs began to expand rapidly in the second half of the 1970s, when baby boomers matured into home-buying age and strongly lifted the demand for housing. As a result, demand for mortgage credit also strengthened substantially. Annual issuance of GNMAs in 1976 jumped to $14 billion, twice the volume of the previous year. By 1983, annual issuance had accelerated to $51 billion. Further, in 1986-87, robust housing activity coupled with the first ever refinancing opportunities made available by sharp declines in mortgage rates skyrocketed GNMAs issuance to almost $100 billion in each year. The slowdown in housing activity and diminished refinancing in 1988-92 cooled off issuance to between $60 and $80 billion annually. But annual issuance of GNMAs accelerated again to nearly $140 billion in 1993, when the housing market revived with a record strong wave of refinancing. In 1994 and 1995, as the refinancing wave receded, GNMAs issuance weakened again to around $110 and $70 billion, respectively. All told, over the 26 years between 1970 and 1995, issuance of GNMAs totaled in excess of $1.2 trillion. As of June 30, 1996, outstanding GNMAs totaled just under $490 billion (Exhibit 2).

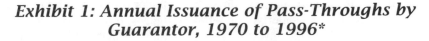

Exhibit 1: Annual Issuance of Pass-Throughs by Guarantor, 1970 to 1996*

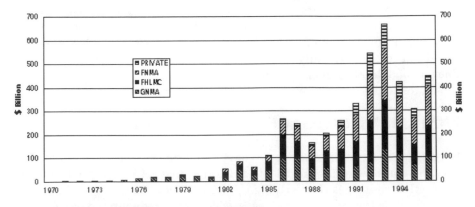

* Figures for 1996 are annualized based on six-month data.

Source: Reprinted with permission of Inside Mortgage Securities, Copyright 1996, Bethesda, Maryland.
(301-951-1240)

Exhibit 2: Outstanding Balance of Mortgage Pass-Throughs by Guarantor, as of June 30, 1996

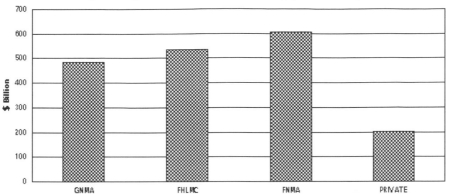

Source: Reprinted with permission of Inside Mortgage Securities, Copyright 1996, Bethesda, Maryland.
(301-951-1240)

Exhibit 3: Features of GNMA I versus GNMA II

Features	GNMA I	GNMA II
Underlying Mortgages	FHA/VA/FmHA mortgages	FHA/VA/FmHA mortgages
Age of Mortgages	Less than 12 months old	Less than 12 months old
Issuer	Single lender	Multiple lenders
Minimum Pool Size	$1,000,000	Jumbo, $250,000 contribution per lender
Range of Underlying Mortgage Rates	All must be the same rate.	Must be within 100 basis points of the lowest mortgage rate in the pool
Servicing Spread	50 basis points	50 to 150 basis points
Method of Payment	One payment per month per pool	One payment per month for all pools from a central paying agent
Payment Date	15th of the month	20th of the month
Stated Payment Delay	44 days	49 days

Source: Ginnie Mae

To facilitate this growth, GNMA initiated a new program in July 1983 to make its pass-throughs more attractive to investors. However, this new program — dubbed GNMA II to differentiate it from the regular program, now called GNMA I — never caught fire in the marketplace. A comparison of the two programs is presented in Exhibit 3. To this day, the majority of GNMAs are issued under GNMA I. These securities are predominantly backed by single-family fixed-rate 30- or 15-year mortgages and one-year adjustable-rate mortgages. A limited number of GNMAs are backed by 30-year fixed-rate graduated-payment mortgages, 15-year mobile home loans, and multi-family construction and permanent financing loans. Major features of GNMAs are presented in Exhibit 4.

Exhibit 4: Major Features of Agency-Guaranteed Pass-Throughs

Feature/ Security Type	GNMA I Pass-Throughs	FHLMC Gold PCs	FNMA MBSs
Issuer	GNMA-approved Seller/servicer	FHLMC	FNMA
Type of Loans	Newly originated FHA/VA/FmHA mortgages	Conventional mortgages and FHA/VA mortgages	Conventional mortgages and FHA/VA mortgages
Guarantor	GNMA	FHLMC	FNMA
Guarantee	Full and timely payment of interest and principal	Full and timely payment of interest and scheduled principal	Full and timely payment of interest and principal
Minimum Delivery (for lender)	$1 million	Regular: $1 million Mini-Guarantor: $250,000	Regular: $250,000 FNMA Major: $250,000
Pool Size (for investor)		Regular: $1 million Giant: $250 million and up	Regular: $1 million Mega: $250 million and up
Mortgage Rate Range	All have the same rate	Guarantor: 0 to 250 basis points Cash: 50 to 100 basis points	0 to 250 basis points
Guarantee Fee	6 basis points	20 to 30 basis points	20 to 30 basis points
Servicing Fees	44 basis points	30 to 35 basis points	30 to 35 basis points
Minimum Investment	$25,000 minimum; $1 increments	$1000 minimum; $1 increments	$1000 minimum; $1 increments
Payment Delivery	Book-entry system for members of Participants Trust Corporation; otherwise physical	Federal Reserve book-entry system	Federal Reserve book-entry system
Payment Date (Stated Payment Delay)	15th of the month following the record date and every month thereafter (44 days)	15th of the month following the record date and every month thereafter (44 days)	25th of the month following the record date and every month thereafter (54 days)
Factor Date	5th business day	1st business day	5th business day
Collateralized Borrowing	Eligible for borrowing at the Federal Reserve's Discount Window	Eligible for borrowing at the Federal Reserve's Discount Window	Eligible for borrowing at the Federal Reserve's Discount Window

Source: Ginnie Mae, Freddie Mac, and Fannie Mae

Concept and Terminology

The concept and terminology of mortgage pass-throughs are unique. For clarification, they are defined below, using GNMAs issued under GNMA I as an example.

The Issuer The issuer of GNMAs is a mortgage lender, not GNMA itself. The lender is most often a mortgage banker. To a limited extent, the issuer can also be a thrift or a commercial bank.

The Guarantor The timely payment of interest and principal on GNMAs is guaranteed by GNMA. This guarantee is backed by the full faith and credit of the U.S. government. Thus, the credit of GNMAs is identical to that of U.S. Treasury securities.

The Seller/Servicer The issuer of the pass-through is by definition the seller of the underlying mortgages of the security. The issuer typically is also the "servicer" of these mortgages. As pointed out in Chapter 2, the function of a servicer includes, among other things, collecting monthly payments from the underlying mortgagors and passing on the cash flow to investors, keeping track of the remaining principal balances of the underlying mortgages, and advancing payments to investors in case of delinquencies and foreclosures.

Uniformity of Underlying Mortgages GNMAs are backed by a pool of newly originated FHA and VA mortgages. To a very limited degree, less than 0.5%, the pool also includes some RHS guaranteed mortgages. All mortgages in the pool have to be less than 12 months of age. They have roughly the same maturity term and carry exactly the same mortgage rate.

Credit Enhancement Although GNMAs are backed by federal government agency insured or guaranteed mortgages, the ultimate credit guarantee of GNMAs is provided by GNMA. In the early years of GNMAs, this credit enhancement greatly improved their acceptance by investors.

The Issue Date and the Maturity Date The issue date simply identifies the actual date of issuance of the pass-through, while the maturity date refers to the longest maturity date of a mortgage in the pool backing the pass-through.

The Factor Date As the underlying mortgages amortize along with the occurrence of prepayments, the outstanding balance of the pool diminishes over time. Thus, on the fifth business day of each month, the factor date, GNMA reports the remaining balance at the end of the previous month of individual pools as a ratio of their respective original balances. This ratio is called *the factor*. For example, as of September 1996, the factor of a specific mortgage pool was 0.81257251. It means that at the end of August 1996, the remaining balance of the pool was 81.257251% of the original balance.

The Record Date and the Payment Date The *record date* determines which investor is entitled to the next scheduled payment of principal and interest of a mortgage pass-through. The actual date when the payment takes place is specified by the *payment date*, which is the 15th day of the month.

The Settlement Date The buyer and the seller of a mortgage pass-through agree on a settlement date when the transacted mortgage pass-through is delivered and the payment for the security is made.

The Weighted Average Coupon The weighted average coupon (WAC) refers to the average interest rate on the mortgages in the pool weighted by the original principal amount of the mortgages. Since the underlying mortgage rates are the same for all regular GNMAs, the weighted average is the simply the uniform mortgage rate. (However, mortgage rates do vary for GNMAs issued under the GNMA II program.)

The Weighted Average Maturity The weighted average maturity (WAM) is the average remaining maturity of the underlying mortgages weighted by the remaining balance of the mortgages.

The Guarantee Fee and the Servicing Fee For the credit guarantee on its pass-throughs, GNMA charges 6 basis points per year from the outstanding balance of the mortgage pool as the guarantee fee. To compensate for the servicing function of the underlying pool, the seller/servicer takes 44 basis points from the outstanding balance of the pool as the servicing fee.

The Pass-Through Coupon Rate For GNMA investors, the coupon rate on the pass-through is the WAC less the guarantee and servicing fees. For example, if the WAC of a GNMA is 8%, the pass-through coupon rate will be 7.5%.

The Delay of First Payment For all mortgages, the monthly interest and the amortized principal are paid in arrears. There is a *30-day standard payment delay* for lenders to receive the first monthly payment. For pass-throughs, there is an additional delay for the servicer to collect monthly payments and pass them to investors. For regular GNMAs, the additional *actual payment delay* is 14 days. Consequently, the *stated payment delay* from the issue date to the first payment date for GNMAs under GNMA I is 44 days (30 plus 14 days).

FREDDIE MAC PARTICIPATION CERTIFICATES

There are two other important types of pass-throughs — Freddie Mac Gold PCs and Fannie Mae MBSs, named after their respective guarantors: *Federal Home Loan Mortgage Corporation* (*Freddie Mac*, hereafter *FHLMC*) and *Federal National Mortgage Association* (*Fannie Mae*, hereafter *FNMA*).

FHLMC was created by Congress in 1970 under the Federal Home Loan Mortgage Corporation Act, Title III of the Emergency Home Finance Act of 1970. As a federally chartered corporation, FHLMC was originally owned by Federal Home Loan Banks. Nearly 20 years later, the Financial Institutions Reform, Recovery, and Enhancement Act of 1989 (FIRREA) converted FHLMC to a private stockholder-owned corporation. However, as a government-sponsored enterprise (GSE), FHLMC is subject to federal government regulation. In fact, three federal agencies have oversight responsibilities over FHLMC's operations: the Office of Federal Housing Enterprise Oversight on its financial safety and soundness, HUD on its housing mission, and the Treasury Department, which must approve its issuance of unsecured debt and new mortgage securities.

One major Congressional mandate of FHLMC has been to provide stability and liquidity to the secondary market for residential mortgages. To fulfill this mandate, FHLMC purchased conventional mortgages from lenders (primarily thrifts, which were members of Federal Home Loan Banks) under the *Cash Program*. To finance these cash purchases, FHLMC simultaneously issued *Participation Certificates* (PCs), which were pass-throughs guaranteed by itself. In the early days, lenders had maintained an undivided *participating* interest in FHLMC guaranteed pass-through *certificates* (thus, the name PCs). However, PCs underwent several program changes that they are now pass-throughs without any participating interest of lenders.

First issued in 1971, PCs went through the same experience as GNMAs in that their annual issuance volume was limited in the early 1970s. It was not until August 1981, when FHLMC initiated the *Guarantor Program*, that issuance of PCs expanded rapidly. The program was to assist thrifts to restructure and improve the liquidity and marketability of their seasoned mortgage portfolios. Under the program, thrifts would swap their holdings of mortgages for FHLMC PCs backed by the same mortgages. The program proved to be an instant success. In 1982, annual issuance of PCs soared to $24 billion. While the program was originally designed to assist thrifts, it quickly evolved to become a viable one to facilitate all lenders in the origination of conventional mortgages.

During the 1980s and the first half of the 1990s, annual issuance of PCs fluctuated in the same pattern as GNMAs (Exhibit 1). It first reached the $100 billion mark in 1986 and established a $200 billion mark in 1993. Total issuance of PCs over the past 16 years exceeded $1.2 trillion. As of June 30, 1996, the outstanding balance of all types of PCs stood at just under $540 billion (Exhibit 2). A great variety of single-family mortgages are now being pooled for PCs. They include: 30- and 15-year fixed-rate, 7- and 5-year balloon, and various adjustable-rate mortgages. More important, in 1990, FHLMC shortened the stated payment delay of PCs from 74 to 44 days (so the payment is made 10 days earlier on the 15th day of the month). The new 44-day pass-throughs are called *Gold PCs*. A detailed description of FHLMC Gold PCs is provided in Exhibit 4.

As a GSE, the guarantee of FHLMC is not backed by the full faith and credit of the U.S. government. However, the long-term debt of FHLMC has been given a triple-A rating from the nation's top credit-rating agencies. Based on FHLMC's GSE status and its top credit rating, investors have viewed the credit of PCs as equal to or better than triple-A.

FANNIE MAE MORTGAGE-BACKED SECURITIES

FNMA was originally created by Congress as a corporation wholly owned by the federal government under the National Housing Act of 1938. The Congressional mandate for FNMA was to help provide liquidity in the secondary market for residential mortgages. It borrowed funds in the capital markets to purchase FHA/VA mortgages originated by mortgage bankers. In 1954, FNMA was reorganized under the Federal National Mortgage Association Charter Act into a "mixed-ownership" corporation partly owned by private stockholders. Further, under the Housing and Urban Development Act of 1968, FNMA was split into two corporations: one was GNMA, which stayed within HUD, and the other was FNMA, which became a private stockholder-owned and operated corporation. FNMA is also a GSE and is subject to the same federal regulation as FHLMC. FNMA also has obtained top credit ratings from rating agencies. Investors generally make no quality distinction between the credit of a FNMA guarantee and that of FHLMC.

Despite its long history as a provider of secondary market liquidity for residential mortgages, FNMA was not a mortgage pass-through guarantor until 1981. Before then, FNMA basically assisted the mortgage market by purchasing mortgages and funded the purchases by issuing its own debt. For this reason, FNMA has always been a much larger corporation than FHLMC in terms of total assets. For example, at yearend 1981, total assets of FNMA were $62 billion. By comparison, assets of FHLMC totaled only $6 billion. In recent years, however, as priorities of operations of both agencies have gradually changed, FHLMC has grown much more rapidly than FNMA. As of yearend 1995, total assets amounted to $317 billion at FNMA and $137 billion at FHLMC.

In December 1981, however, FNMA entered the pass-through market by commencing a *FNMA MBS Program* to assist thrifts. In essence, the mechanics of the program were similar to FHLMC's Guarantor Program: thrifts sell mortgages to FNMA and in return receive FNMA guaranteed pass-throughs backed by precisely the same mortgages. The MBS program also underwent several design changes to facilitate all mortgage originations. Now, FNMAs are essentially backed by newly originated conventional mortgages of various types (Exhibit 4). They include 30- and 15-year fixed-rate mortgages, 7-year balloon mortgages (FNMAs do not include 5-year balloons), and adjustable rate mortgages of a variety of indexes.

During the 1980s, annual issuance of FNMAs was almost always smaller than that of FHLMCs. This pattern, however, reversed in the 1990s. In 1990, issuance of FNMAs almost topped $100 billion, surpassing FHLMCs by over $20 billion. In 1993, issuance of FNMAs set a record at $220 billion. Between 1991 and 1994, issuance of FNMAs stayed consistently above $100 billion. While FNMA entered the pass-through market 11 years after GNMA and FHLMC, total issuance of FNMAs over the past 15 years still exceeded $1.2 trillion. As of June 30, 1996, there were slightly over $600 billion FNMAs outstanding, $120 and $70 billion more than GNMAs and FHLMCs, respectively (Exhibits 1 and 2).

PRIVATE-LABEL PASS-THROUGHS

Mortgages that are pooled for FHLMC Gold PCs or FNMA MBSs are conforming to the program specifics of mortgage securitization at the two guarantors (FNMA and FHLMC). One important feature of these *conforming mortgages* is the size of the original loan balance. Currently, for single-family mortgages, the conforming limit is $207,000. Mortgages that exceed this limit are not eligible for inclusion in agency-guaranteed pass-throughs. However, lenders can still package *non-conforming* (or *jumbo*) *mortgages* to issue *private-label pass-throughs* (or simply private pass-throughs to distinguish them from agency pass-throughs).

Private pass-throughs were first issued in 1977 by the Bank of America. In almost 20 years, more than $400 billion of private pass-throughs have been issued. As of June 30, 1996, their outstanding balance topped $200 billion. As will be discussed in Chapter 7, private pass-throughs are rarely issued in one maturity class. Almost invariably, they are issued as REMICs in the form of multiple maturity classes. Private pass-throughs have become increasingly important in recent years, and Chapter 8 will be devoted to a detailed discussion of these securities.

CURRENT TRADING OF PASS-THROUGHS

The market for agency-guaranteed fixed-rate mortgage pass-throughs (hereafter, pass-throughs) is a mature one. Like Treasuries, pass-throughs are traded almost around the clock in New York, London, and Tokyo. (The discussion here focuses on fixed-rate pass-throughs. Chapter 4 presents trading of adjustable rate mortgage pass-throughs.) Dozens of Wall Street dealers and brokers are constantly buying and selling (making markets) in billions dollars of pass-throughs.

TBA Trades

Pass-throughs trade on either a *to-be-announced* (TBA) or a *specified basis* in terms of the identification of the underlying pools of mortgages. TBA trading is necessary for newly issued pass-throughs because at the point of sale the seller (mortgage originators) cannot be certain as to the precise characteristics of the underlying pool of mortgages. For example, because mortgage rates are constantly changing, the seller has no control over how many loans that are committed to originate will eventually be originated. The seller, however, can specify the coupon rate, the type (GNMA, FNMA, or FHLMC), and the face amount of the pass-through to be sold. Based on these specifications, a newly issued pass-through can be traded at a price according to market conditions.

Forward Settlement

Since the origination of mortgages is a time-consuming process, a TBA trade of new pass-through can only be settled on a forward basis. The forward settlement is at least one month after the trade has taken place, and it can be up to four months. The forward settlement dates are scheduled by a calendar published by the Public Securities Association. The calendar is announced quarterly for the upcoming six months. Forty-eight hours before the settlement date, the seller has to provide the buyer with information on the characteristics of the mortgage pool. To the extent that the seller cannot deliver to the buyer precisely the original principal amount of pass-throughs sold, three separate pools per $1 million of original principal with a variance of plus or minus 1% are allowed. Meeting these stipulations constitutes a *good delivery*.

Specified Trades

Existing pass-throughs, where the pool information is readily identifiable by their cusip numbers, are traded on a specified basis. For specified trades, the seller specifies the coupon, the original face amount, and the WAM. Trades usually settle after new pool factors are released. However, they can also settle on a same-day, Treasury (one business-day), or corporate (three business-day) basis. Because they are specified trades, they do not have to follow the rules of good delivery. The seller and the buyer can negotiate the variance. It can be greater than 1% or none at all.

Bid-Offer Price Spreads

Given that market conditions remain unchanged, the liquidity of a security is reflected by the difference between the purchase (bid) and the selling (offer) prices of the security. Understandably, this is a narrow definition of liquidity. In a broader sense, a security of "true liquidity" is when its price is virtually unaffected by the changing market conditions. Nevertheless, in a narrow sense, pass-throughs are liquid. The bid-offer spread of newly issued pass-throughs of current and discount coupons (30-year 6.5s to 7.5s and 15-year 6s to 7s in today's market of an 8% fixed mortgage rate) is merely $\frac{1}{32}$ of a point, or 1 tick. This spread applies only to a round lot with a minimal current principal of $1 million. For an odd lot of current principal less than $1 million, the bid-offer spread is significantly greater than 1 tick. For deep-discount coupons (30-year 6s), the bid-offer spread could widen to 2 ticks; for high premium coupons (30-year 9s and above), 4 ticks. For balloon pass-throughs, the bid-offer spread is generally 2 ticks.

Chapter 4

Mortgage Prepayment

- Definition of Prepayment and Prepayment Rate
- Measurements of Prepayment Rate
- Two Fundamental Reasons for Prepayments
- Impact on Relative Value of Mortgage Pass-Throughs
- Modeling Prepayment

DEFINITION OF PREPAYMENT AND PREPAYMENT RATE

While a mortgage is a long-term debt, the mortgagor can retire the debt before maturity. This early retirement of a mortgage debt is called *prepayment*. Mortgages are almost always prepayable at par without any penalties. Because mortgages amortize, the outstanding principal balance of a mortgage pass-through diminishes over time even when none of the underlying mortgages is prepaid. Since most mortgagors prepay, the outstanding balance of a mortgage pass-through diminishes much more rapidly than its scheduled amortization. *Thus, prepayment is defined as only the paydown of the outstanding balance of a mortgage pass-through that is in excess of its scheduled amortization.* The speed of the excess paydown is measured by the *prepayment rate*. The prepayment rate is unique to mortgage pass-throughs and is the most important factor in determining their value relative to other fixed-income securities, such as Treasuries and corporate bonds.

MEASUREMENTS OF PREPAYMENT RATE

Prepayment is the paydown of principal of a mortgage pass-through in a given month that exceeds the amount of its scheduled amortization for that month. The rate of prepayment is therefore the excessive paydown in a given month as a percent of the outstanding principal balance at the beginning of the month. This excess paydown is always measured on a monthly basis. Like interest rates, however, it is often expressed as an annualized rate. The prepayment rate of a mortgage pool is low right after its formation, but it accelerates as the pool ages. In the initial years, therefore, the prepayment rate is often measured in conjunction with the aging of the pool.

Single Month Mortality

Single month mortality (SMM) rate measures the percentage of a pool's outstanding balance at the beginning of the month that was prepaid during the month. Algebraically, the SMM of month N, SMM_N, is calculated with the following formulas:

expressed in an annualized rate rather than the monthly rate. The conversion is based on the formula,

$$CPR = 1 - (1 - SMM)^{12}$$

and consists of the following steps:

Step 1. Given the single month mortality rate, the "survival rate" is simply $(1 - SMM)$. From the above example, the monthly survival rate is $(1 - 0.007828) = 0.992172$

Step 2. Given the monthly survival rate of 0.992172, the annualized survival rate is $(0.992172)^{12} = 0.910005 = 91\%$

Step 3. Since an annualized 91% of the pool survived in the 60th month, the annualized rate of prepayment of the pool in the 60th month is

$$CPR = [1 - (1 - SMM)^{12}] = 1 - (0.992172)^{12} = 1 - 0.910005$$
$$= 0.089995 = 9\%$$

Public Securities Association Standard

To measure the paydown of a mortgage pool with respect to its age, the Public Securities Association (PSA) promulgated a new yardstick termed "percent PSA." As shown in Exhibit 1, a 100% PSA refers to a pool that prepays (1) at a 0.2% CPR in the first month, (2) at a faster rate of incrementally 0.2% CPR per month during the first 30 months, and (3) at a constant 6% CPR per month at the 31st month and thereafter. The first 30 months of the PSA curve is sometimes called "the ramp period." For a given month, a pool may prepay faster or slower than this standard. Its prepayment speed is expressed as a multiple or a fraction of PSA. (Colloquially, the prepayment rate is often called "the prepayment speed," or simply "the speed.")

Exhibit 1: Prepayment Measured by PSAs

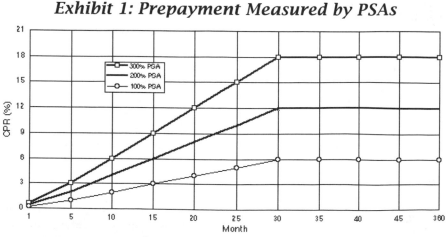

Source: Public Securities Association

From the above example, given that the CPR for the 60th month is 9%, the PSA speed for that month is 9%/6% = 150% PSA. However, if the 9% CPR occurs for the 20th month, then the speed would be 100 × [9% / (0.2 × 20)] = 225% PSA. For the same CPR, the reason that the PSA speed is faster for the 20th month than for the 60th month is that the PSA standard expects a 20-month-old pool to prepay only 6% CPR on a 150% PSA. The fact that it already prepays at 9% CPR, the PSA standard adjusts the speed upward to 225% PSA.

Given the age of a mortgage pool, the following formulas convert interchangeably between CPR and PSA:

When the age of a mortgage pool is younger that 30 months:

$$PSA = 100 \times [CPR/(0.2 \times age)]$$

$$CPR = (PSA \times 0.2 \times age)/100$$

When the age of a mortgage pool is 30 months or older:

$$PSA = 100 \times (CPR/6)$$

$$CPR = (PSA \times 6)/100$$

TWO FUNDAMENTAL REASONS FOR PREPAYMENT

A mortgage is originated as a long-term finance instrument to finance the purchase of a home. However, for a variety of reasons, the mortgagor rarely holds onto the mortgage until its maturity. There are two fundamental reasons that a mortgage is prepaid: refinancing and housing turnover. Housing turnover can be the result of mortgage default, disaster, or death of the mortgagor.

Refinancing

In a declining interest rate environment, the mortgagor has a strong incentive to refinance. That is, the mortgagor would prepay the existing mortgage that carries an above-market rate and obtain a new mortgage at the market rate. By refinancing, the mortgagor reduces the monthly payment. Thus, refinancing is an important reason for prepayment. In 1993, for example, when mortgage rates plunged below 7%, their lowest level in 25 years, refinancing became rampant. Nearly one-half of that year's $1.1 trillion of mortgage originations were the result of refinancing. It amounted to 18% of all outstanding mortgages in 1993.

Housing Turnover

Prepayment occurs even when interest rates are stable. Absent refinancing, a mortgage is prepaid as a result of a change in the ownership of its collateral—the house. The ownership change may be the result of home sale, default, disaster (such as fire, flood, or earthquake), or death of the mortgagor.

Home Sale The primary cause of the ownership change is the mortgagor selling the house for a variety of reasons. They include, but are not limited to, upgrading housing, changing job, or divorce. A conventional mortgage (not insured or guaranteed by government) normally has a due-on-sale clause, which requires the mortgagor to prepay when the house is sold. While a FHA/VA mortgage allows the buyer to take over the mortgage from the seller (termed mortgage assumption), the seller usually still prepays the mortgage.

Default The financial condition of the mortgagor may deteriorate such that he or she is no longer able to carry the monthly payment. If the condition is temporary, the mortgage is said to be in "delinquency." However, if the inability to pay persists for more than three months, the mortgage would be in "default." In this case, the lender can initiate a foreclosure proceeding, which eventually will liquidate the house and pay off the mortgage. It is important to note, however, that mortgages traditionally have a very low incidence of default. In recent years, the average annual rate of default has been less than 0.5%.

Disaster A mortgage may also be prepaid as a result of severe damage to the house because of fire, flood, or earthquake. Since the house is the collateral that secures the mortgage, severe damage to the collateral eliminates the very existence of the mortgage. If the house has casualty insurance, the mortgage will be prepaid. If not, the mortgage usually ends up in default.

Death In case of death of the mortgagor, the executor usually sells the house and prepays the mortgage. Otherwise, if the mortgage becomes defaulted, the lender will foreclose the house and prepay the mortgage.

IMPACT ON RELATIVE VALUE OF MORTGAGE PASS-THROUGHS

Since mortgages are always prepaid at par, prepayment adds value to discount-coupon mortgage pass-throughs — those that are priced below par. Conversely, for premium coupons — those priced above par — prepayment subtracts value. As interest rates change, however, the magnitude of this impact varies.

Discount Coupons

In a rising interest rate environment, prepayment slows down due to the weakening of housing activity. As a consequence, the positive impact of prepayment on discount coupons is mitigated. Conversely, in a declining interest rate environment, as housing activity strengthens, the acceleration of prepayment adds value to discount coupons. If interest rates decline substantially, even discount coupons will experience refinancing. This further magnifies the positive impact of prepayment on discount coupons.

Premium Coupons

As interest rates rise, prepayment will decline due to the diminishing opportunities for refinancing and the slowdown of housing activity. Both reduce the negative impact of prepayment on premium coupons. On the other hand, if interest rates decline, prepayment will rise because refinancing accelerates and housing activity gains strength. Accelerated refinancing and strengthened housing will accentuate the negative impact of prepayment on premium coupons.

MODELING PREPAYMENT

Mortgage pass-throughs are unique fixed-income securities due to prepayment caused by a variety of unpredictable events. Because of the unpredictability of these events, mortgage securities have uncertain cash flows. Given prices but with uncertain cash flows, the yields of mortgage pass-throughs can only be estimated under a set of assumptions of future prepayment. The estimated yields can only be realistic if the assumptions prove to be close to reality.

Thus, over the past 15 years, the focus of mortgage research has been to identify the determinants of prepayment. These determinants generally have been identified through econometric models (multiple regression equations). Based on these models, researchers have attempted to project future prepayment. The projections are then incorporated in the yield calculation of mortgage pass-throughs. In general, the following determinants have been identified by most regression equations as having significant influence on prepayment.

Difference between the WAC and the Market Mortgage Rates

Refinancing has been identified as one of the most important events affecting the prepayment of a mortgage pool. It takes place when the WAC of the pool exceeds market mortgage rates. The excess, or the "refinancing threshold," has become increasingly small through time. Competition among mortgage bankers and advanced computer technology have constantly lowered the cost of mortgage originations and diminished the refinancing threshold. Nowadays, a moderate decline in market mortgage rates can trigger a significant wave of refinancing.

Housing Turnover Rate

Another important determinant of prepayment is housing activity, measured by the housing turnover rate — a ratio of existing home sales to the stock of occupied single-family houses. Exhibit 2 presents annual sales of existing homes and the housing turnover rate between 1980 and 1995. For convenience, the turnover rate is also expressed in terms of PSA speeds. In 1995, for example, annual existing home sales totaled 3.802 million units and the housing stock was estimated at 63.7 million units. The housing turnover rate therefore was 6%. Interestingly, in the parlance of prepayment, this turnover rate converts precisely to a 100% PSA.

Exhibit 2: Annual Sales of Existing Homes, Stock of Occupied Single-Family Houses, and Housing Turnover Rate, 1980 to 1995

Year	Sales of Existing Homes (millions of units)	Occupied Single-Family Housing Stock (millions of units)	Housing Turnover Rate (%)	Housing Turnover Rate Expressed in % PSA
1980	2.973	51.6	5.8	96
1981	2.419	52.8	4.6	76
1982	1.991	54.0	3.7	61
1983	2.697	55.0	4.9	82
1984	2.829	56.1	5.0	84
1985	3.134	57.2	5.5	91
1986	3.474	58.0	6.0	100
1987	3.436	58.9	5.8	97
1988	3.513	59.9	5.9	98
1989	3.346	60.9	5.5	92
1990	3.211	61.4	5.2	87
1991	3.220	61.9	5.2	87
1992	3.520	62.3	5.7	94
1993	3.802	62.6	6.1	101
1994	3.946	62.9	6.3	105
1995	3.802	63.7	6.0	100

Notes: Annual occupied single-family housing stock is first estimated from a five-year moving average of housing stock of all types to smooth out the fluctuation due to different surveys. The moving average is then multiplied by 0.67 to arrive at the estimate of single-family stock.

Sources: National Association of Realtors and U.S. Bureau of the Census

For discount and current coupon pass-throughs, whose WACs are below the market mortgage rate, the housing turnover rate is the major factor determining their prepayment rates. Exhibit 3 compares the housing turnover rate with prepayment rates of 30-year GNMAs and FNMAs between 1983 and 1995. (Prepayments of discount and current coupons are shaded, with current coupon prepayments in bold face.) With the exception of 1986-87 and 1992-93, when refinancing was strong, the housing turnover rate accounted for the bulk of prepayments of discount and current coupons. For GNMAs, prepayment during the 1983-85 period was exceedingly slow. It was far below the housing turnover rate because historically high mortgage rates in the early 1980s encouraged many buyers of FHA/VA financed homes to assume the underlying mortgages. This was called "mortgage assumption." With mortgage assumption, sales of existing homes were accounted for in the housing turnover rate but not in prepayment. Based on Exhibit 3, it is reasonable to assume that mortgage pass-throughs have a minimum prepayment of around 100% PSA.

Exhibit 3: Annual Average Prepayment Rates of Seasoned Production
30-Year Pass-Throughs, Selected Coupons, 1986-95

Year	Housing Turnover Rate (% PSA)	GNMAs (WAMs shorter than 330 months, in %PSA)						
		7%	7.5%	8%	8.5%	9%	9.5%	10%
1983	82	80	47	50	57	43	41	46
1984	84	77	42	45	52	40	39	43
1985	91	93	60	64	69	55	53	56
1986	100	123	120	122	131	119	123	131
1987	97	141	129	133	144	143	160	198
1988	98	129	108	114	123	124	134	144
1989	92	107	101	102	110	111	121	130
1990	87	86	101	98	84	93	116	133
1991	87	65	84	86	93	109	141	196
1992	94	71	127	135	173	266	427	534
1993	101	105	209	292	527	639	730	707
1994	105	110	170	219	354	398	475	521
1995	100	104	132	155	198	226	265	287

Year	Housing Turnover Rate (% PSA)	FNMAs (WAMs shorter than 330 months, in % PSA)						
		7%	7.5%	8%	8.5%	9%	9.5%	10%
1983	82	105	101	87	113	112	107	108
1984	84	110	104	91	120	127	116	129
1985	91	120	117	104	129	137	149	153
1986	100	132	160	146	182	197	238	265
1987	97	138	171	155	199	200	275	321
1988	98	129	135	128	149	162	192	200
1989	92	123	124	113	133	138	157	170
1990	87	124	124	110	125	129	143	156
1991	87	150	145	129	154	177	227	297
1992	94	231	265	266	398	600	769	772
1993	101	221	396	570	772	872	814	690
1994	105	114	216	302	402	475	500	498
1995	100	90	109	139	190	247	274	282

Note: Shaded areas represent discount- and current-coupon prepayment rates

Source: Oppenheimer & Co., Inc.

Age

As demonstrated through the PSA curve, the prepayment of a newly originated mortgage pool (a new pool) tends to rise slowly but steadily during the first two and a half years (the ramp period) after its formation. As the pool ages beyond the ramp period (becoming a seasoned pool), its prepayment generally levels off. This is a housing-related phenomenon. At the current level of mortgage rates and housing activity, prepayments of new pools level off at around 6% to 8% CPR. This pattern describes a typical situation where new home owners usually stay put after moving into a new home, although they become more likely to move over time. Various surveys conducted by the U. S. Bureau of the Census indicated that on average 5% to 7% of home owners move annually during the first three years. By the 10th to 12th years, 50% of home owners have moved.

From the risk point of view, however, a new pool tends to show a sporadic prepayment behavior. As shown in Exhibits 4 and 5, prepayment rates of new production and seasoned 30-year GNMA and FNMA 7s were far more volatile than their seasoned counterparts. One major reason for the volatility in prepayment is error in mortgage underwriting. Poorly underwritten mortgages tend to have high incidence of default in the initial years. These defaults account for the bulk of prepayments of new pools. By contrast, as mortgage pools become seasoned, defaults represent an increasingly insignificant portion of prepayments.

Exhibit 4: Prepayment of New Production and Seasoned 30-Year GNMA7s and Fixed Mortgage Rates
1/90 to 6/96

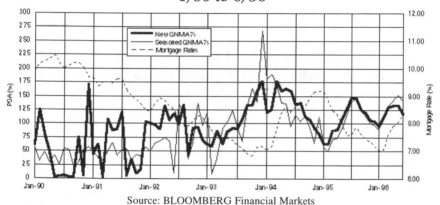

Source: BLOOMBERG Financial Markets

Exhibit 5: Prepayment of New Production and Seasoned 30-Year FNMA 7s and FIxed Mortgage Rates
1/90 to 6/96

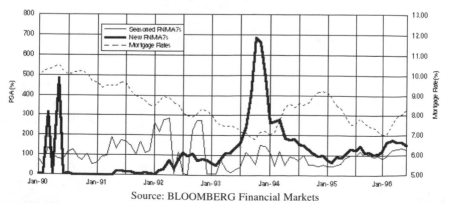

Source: BLOOMBERG Financial Markets

Exhibit 6: Prepayment of New Production and Seasoned 30-Year GNMA 9s and Fixed Mortgage Rates
1/90 to 6/96

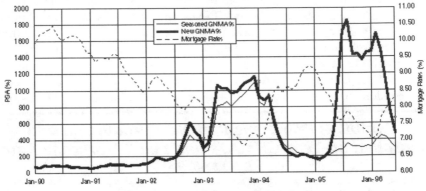

Source: BLOOMBERG Financial Markets

Exhibit 7: Prepayment of New Production and Seasoned 30-Year FNMA 9s and Fixed Mortgage Rates
1/90 to 6/96

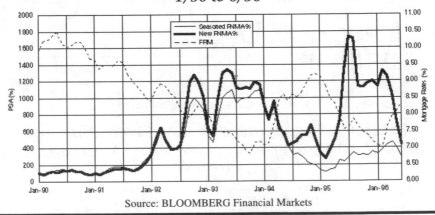

Source: BLOOMBERG Financial Markets

Age also affects the refinancing aspect of prepayment. Newly originated mortgage pools tend to be far more sensitive to declines in mortgage rates than seasoned pools. For example, the prepayment rate of seasoned 30-year GNMA 9s (WAM: 240 months) accelerated from below 200% PSA in mid-1992 to above 800% PSA in late-1993 when mortgage rates first dropped to 7% (Exhibits 6 and 7). However, during most of 1995, when mortgage rates hovered again around 7%, seasoned GNMA 9s prepaid below 300% PSA. A similar pattern also exists for seasoned FNMA 9s. This demonstrates that seasoned pools, with interest-rate sensitive mortgagors already refinanced, are far less sensitive to declines in mortgage rates than their new production counterparts.

Exhibit 8: Prepayment of New Production and Seasoned 30-Year GNMA 8s and Fixed Mortgage Rates
1/90 to 6/96

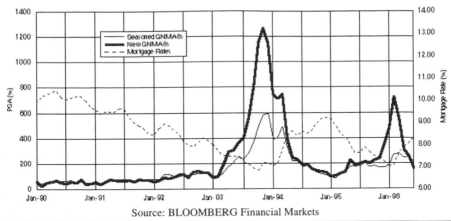

Source: BLOOMBERG Financial Markets

Seasonality

Since housing activity fluctuates seasonally, the prepayment of a mortgage pool also exhibits a seasonal pattern, rising in the spring and summer and declining in the fall and winter. Seasonality is more significant for discount and current coupons than for premium coupons.

Shape of the Treasury Yield Curve

The shape of the Treasury yield curve affects the prepayment of a mortgage pool in two ways. First, in a steeper yield curve environment, adjustable-rate mortgages (ARMs) usually carry significantly lower initial rates than fixed rate mortgages (FRMs). In such an environment, prepayment tends to rise because mortgagors have a stronger incentive to refinance their FRMs with ARMs. Second, when short-term rates are substantially lower than long-term rates, mortgagors have a tendency to use their short-term investments to pay off a portion of their mortgages. This phenomenon is called *curtailment*. Curtailment reduces the outstanding principal balance of a pool faster than amortization, but not as much as prepayment.

Burnout

Prepayment tends to rise far more dramatically when mortgage rates first drop below the refinancing threshold than they do in the second or third round of declining rates. This "burnout" phenomenon typically happens among newly originated mortgage pools. For example, Exhibit 8 shows that the prepayment rate of new production 30-year GNMA 8s (WAM: 340 months) surged above 1200% PSA in late 1993, when mortgage rates first plunged to 7% (also Exhibit 9 for 30-

year FNMA 8s). In early 1996, when mortgage rates dropped backed to 7% again, the prepayment rate of GNMA 8s hovered only around 700% PSA. This phenomenon suggests that even for new production pools, the responsiveness of refinancing gradually "burns out" in each new round of declining mortgage rates.

Exhibit 9: Prepayment of New Production and Seasoned 30-Year FNMA 8s and FIxed Mortgage Rates
1/90 to 6/96

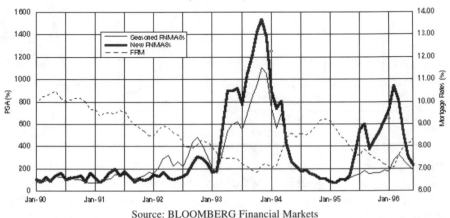

Source: BLOOMBERG Financial Markets

Chapter 5

Basic Mortgage Math

- Amortizing a Mortgage
- Projecting the Cash Flow of a Pool of Mortgages
- Mortgage Yield versus Bond Equivalent Yield
- Expected Average Life
- Mortgage Yield Spread
- Duration
- Convexity
- Option Adjusted Analysis

AMORTIZING A MORTGAGE

As mentioned in Chapter 1, a mortgage debt is amortized by a gradual paydown of the original principal along with the interest payment on the remaining principal throughout the term of the mortgage. The monthly payment of the mortgage is constant, although the mix of principal paydown and interest payment varies.

Algebraically, the monthly payment is determined by the following formula:

$$OPB = MP/(1 + R/12)^1 + MP/(1 + R/12)^2 + \ldots + MP/(1 + R/12)^N$$

where

OPB	=	original principal balance
MP	=	monthly payment
R	=	annual mortgage rate
$R/12$	=	monthly mortgage rate
N	=	month 1, 2, ..., N, which goes to 360 for a 30-year mortgage

The formula basically states that the sum of the present value of all future monthly payments, which are discounted by the monthly mortgage rate, is equal to the original principal balance. Given an annual mortgage rate, the monthly payment can be calculated by rearranging the above formula into the following form:

$$MP = OPB \times \{[(R/12) \times (1 + R/12)^N]/[(1 + R/12)^N - 1]\}$$

For example, a 30-year mortgage with an original principal balance of $100,000 at an 8% annual mortgage rate will have a constant monthly payment of $733.76.

That is:

$$MP = 100,000 \times \{[(0.08/12) \times (1 + 0.08/12)^{360}] / [(1 + 0.08/12)^{360} - 1]\}$$
$$=100,000 \times \{[(0.006667) \times 10.935731] / [10.935731 - 1]\}$$
$$=100,000 \times \{0.72909 / 9.935731\} = 733.76$$

Out of the constant monthly payment of \$733.76, the interest payment of the first month will be \$100,000 × (0.08/12), or \$666.67. The paydown of principal for the first month will be \$733.76 − \$666.67 = \$67.09. For the second month, the interest payment will be slightly smaller because of the modest paydown or "amortization" of principal in the first month. So, the second interest payment is (\$100,000 − \$67.09) × (0.08/12) = \$666.22. The paydown of principal in the second month will be \$733.76 − \$666.22 = \$67.54, which is slightly larger than that of the first month. This process continues with a modestly rising principal paydown and declining interest payment. Toward the end of the maturity term of the mortgage, the interest payment will become increasingly negligible with the bulk of the monthly payment being principal paydown. At the end of the 30th year, the mortgage will be completely paid off.

PROJECTING THE CASH FLOW OF A POOL OF MORTGAGES

While the scheduled monthly payment of a mortgage is algebraically certain, that of a pool of mortgages is not due to prepayment. To analyze the value of a mortgage security backed by a pool of mortgages, its future cash flow has to be *projected under certain prepayment assumptions*. Throughout this chapter, the mortgage math of mortgage securities is illustrated using generic new production 30-year Ginnie Mae 7.5s (hereafter GNMA 7.5s) as an example.

In mid-1996, when mortgage rates were hovering around 8%, newly originated FHA/VA mortgages carried a note rate of 8%. They were pooled for the issuance of GNMA 7.5s, making them the current production coupon of pass-throughs. Typically, the current production coupon is the highest discount coupon that is priced closest to but below par. As of May 30, 1996, GNMA 7.5s were priced at 98%/32 for June settlement, the highest discount price among all 30-year GNMAs.

To analyze the value of GNMA 7.5s, certain assumptions need to be made regarding their future prepayment. Given prevailing mortgage rates in mid-1996, the market assumed that GNMA 7.5s would prepay at a long-term speed of 130% PSA. It should be noted that the prepayment rate of a pass-through is rarely constant. However, the assumption of a constant prepayment rate makes it easier to conduct the analysis. Exhibit 1 provides the projected monthly cash flow of selected months of generic new production GNMA 7.5s with a WAM of 355 months (age: 5 months). Exhibit 2 presents the projected monthly cash flow of the entire 355 months of GNMA 7.5s under a 130% PSA. Notice that in both Exhibits 1 and 2, the steadily rising cash flow from the first to the 25th month reflects the gradual rise in prepayment as the underlying mortgage pool ages (the PSA ramp).

Exhibit 1: Projected Cash Flow of Selected Months of Generic New 30-Year GNMA 7.5s
Assumed Prepayment Rate: 130% PSA
WAM: 355 Months
Original Principal Balance: $100,000

Month	Remaining Balance	Interest Payment	Amortized Payment	Prepaid Principal	Total Principal Paydown	Total Cash Flow
0	$100,000.00					
1	99,799.55	$625.00	$69.60	$130.85	200.45	$825.45
2	99,577.04	623.75	69.97	152.53	222.51	846.25
3	99,332.57	622.36	70.33	174.14	244.48	866.83
24	89,430.75	563.07	74.34	586.15	660.49	1,223.56
25	88,753.72	558.94	74.35	602.68	677.03	1,235.97
26	88,081.27	554.71	74.34	598.11	672.45	1,227.16
353	143.28	1.35	71.41	0.97	72.38	73.73
354	71.39	0.90	71.40	0.48	71.89	72.78
355	0	0.44	71.39	0	71.39	71.83

Source: BLOOMBERG Financial Markets

Exhibit 2: Projected Cash Flow of 30-Year GNMA 7.5s at 130% PSA, Original Principal: $100,000 WAM: 355 months

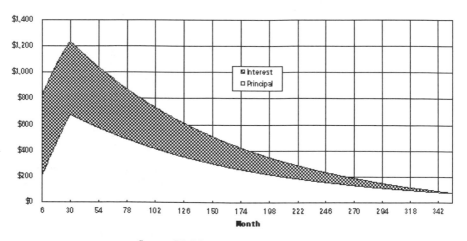

Source: BLOOMBERG Financial Markets

MORTGAGE YIELD VERSUS BOND EQUIVALENT YIELD

Given the price and the projected cash flow, Exhibit 3 shows a Bloomberg Mortgage screen of a "quick yield analysis" of generic new production GNMA 7.5s. It shows that, as of May 30, 1996, GNMA 7.5s were priced at 98⁸⁄₃₂. Under an assumed prepayment speed of 130% PSA, they had a *mortgage yield* of 7.74%.

Because a mortgage pass-through is a monthly-pay instrument, its yield is computed on a *monthly compounding* basis. The yield is basically the discount rate that converts the future monthly cash flow of the security (made up of amortized principal, prepayment, and interest payment) into a present value. The discount rate is obtained through an iterative calculation. By trail and error, a correct discount rate is obtained to satisfy the present value equation. The ratio of the present value to the original principal balance is the price of the security. Algebraically, given the price of a mortgage security, its yield is derived from the following formula:

$$PR = 100 \times PV / OPB$$

$$PV = CF_1 / (1 + Y/12)^{1-1+d/30} + CF_2 / (1 + Y/12)^{2-1+d/30}$$
$$+ \ldots + CF_N / (1 + Y/12)^{N-1+d/30}$$

where

PV	= present value of all future monthly cash flow of pass-through
OPB	= original principal balance of pass-through
PR	= market price of pass-through, expressed as a percent of OPB
CF_N	= monthly cash flow of principal and interest payment of month N
$(1 + Y/12)^N$	= discount factor for month N
d	= days of stated delay of first payment
Y	= annual mortgage yield of mortgage pass-through
$Y/12$	= monthly mortgage yield of mortgage pass-through
N	= month 1, 2, ..., N, which in the present case goes to month 355

The market price of 98⁸⁄₃₂ means that the projected future cash flow of GNMA 7.5s, when discounted by an appropriate discount rate, has a present value of $98,250. The projected monthly cash flow in Exhibit 1 is applied to the above formula:

$$98250 = 825.45 / (1 + Y/12)^{1-1+44/30} + 846.25 / (1 + Y/12)^{2-1+44/30} + \ldots$$
$$+ 74.84 / (1 + Y/12)^{355-1+44/30}$$

Through an iterative process, the discount rate is calculated to be 0.00645, or 0.645%. Thus, the annual "mortgage yield" of GNMA 7.5s is $12 \times 0.00645 = 0.074$, or 7.74%.

To compare the value of a mortgage security with a Treasury or a corporate bond, both of which are semi-annual-pay instruments, the mortgage yield is often converted to a *bond equivalent yield (BEY)*. The conversion follows a simple formula:

$$BEY = 2 \times [(1 + Y/12)^6 - 1]$$

Exhibit 3 shows that the BEY for GNMA 7.5s is 7.866%, 12.6 basis points higher than the mortgage yield. This difference is called "add-on." The add-on is not constant; it varies according to the level of mortgage yield. For example, Exhibit 4 shows that at a 7% mortgage yield, the add-on is 10 basis points. It increases to 28 basis points when mortgage yield rises to 11.5%. The reason for the add-on is that monthly compounding yields more than semi-annual compounding. For a fair comparison between the monthly-pay mortgage securities and semi-annual pay securities, mortgage yields need to be adjusted upward with an add-on to bond equivalent yields.

Exhibit 3: Quick Yield Analysis of Generic 30-Year GNMA 7.5s
(A Screen of Bloomberg Mortgage Analytics)

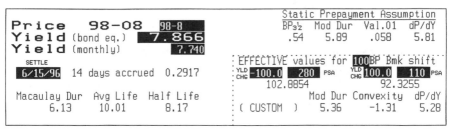

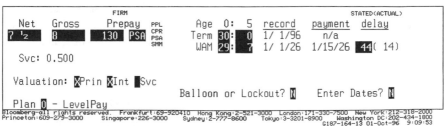

Source: BLOOMBERG Financial Markets

Exhibit 4: Add-on Factor for a Selected Range of Mortgage Yields

Mortgage Yield (%)	Bond Eq. Yield (%)	Add-on Factor (bp)	Mortgage Yield (%)	Bond Eq. Yield (%)	Add-on Factor (bp)
6.0	6.076	7.6	9.0	9.170	17.0
6.5	6.589	8.9	9.5	9.690	19.0
7.0	7.103	10.3	10.0	10.211	21.1
7.5	7.618	11.8	10.5	10.732	23.2
8.0	8.135	13.5	11.0	11.255	25.5
8.5	8.652	15.2	11.5	11.779	27.9

EXPECTED AVERAGE LIFE

Average life is the dollar-weighted average time to receive payment of principal. This concept is important to mortgage pass-throughs because their cash flows include the return of principal as a result of both scheduled amortization and prepayment. The average life for mortgage securities is described as "expected" because their cash flows can only be projected with prepayment assumptions. The interim return of principal before maturity makes average lives of mortgage securities significantly shorter than their maturities. By contrast, for Treasury securities and corporate bonds, where the principal is returned at maturity, average life is the same as maturity.

Given an assumed prepayment speed and the resulting principal payment, the expected average life (AL) of a pass-through is computed with the following formula:

$$AL = \{(1 \times P_1) + (2 \times P_2) + ... + (N \times P_N)\} / (12 \times OPB)$$

where

P_N = principal balance returned at month N
OPB = original principal balance
N = month elapsed from settlement date to the actual receipt of principal, which goes from 1, 2, ..., to N (for a brand new 30-year pass-through, N is 360)

By applying the projected cash flow in Exhibit 1 to the above formula, the expected average life of generic new production GNMA 7.5s is only 10.01 years, although their WAM is 355 months, or 29.6 years. The average life is computed as follows:

$$AL = \{(1 \times 200.45) + (2 \times 222.51) + ... + (355 \times 71.39)\} / (12 \times 100000)$$
$$= \{200.45 + 445.01 + ... + 25344.06\} / (12 \times 100000)$$
$$= 12009518.87 / (12 \times 100000)$$
$$= 10.01$$

From the above formula, if the prepayment speed of GNMA 7.5s accelerates to 200% PSA, the average life would shorten markedly to 7.6 years. This is because a greater portion of the paydown in the early years will be assigned a smaller weight. To illustrate, consider a simple example: a three-year pass-through of an original principal of $120. It has a slow prepayment speed with an expected annual principal paydown of $30, $40, and $50. In this case, its average life is [1 × $30 + 2 × $40 + 3 × $50)] / $120 = 2.17 years. However, if its principal payment schedule quickens to $50, $40, and $30, its average life would be shortened to [10 × $50 + 2 × $40 +3 × $30)] / $120 = 1.83 years.

MORTGAGE YIELD SPREAD

For analysis of relative value of mortgage pass-throughs, their yields are typically compared to those of Treasury securities. Since the maturity of a Treasury security is also its average life, a mortgage pass-through is typically compared to a "comparable average life" Treasury security. Typically, the yield of a pass-through is markedly higher than the yield of its comparable Treasury security. This difference is "mortgage yield spread," or simply "yield spread."

For example, Exhibit 5 shows that on May 30, 1996, at a price of 98⁸⁄32, the bond equivalent yield of GNMA 7.5s was 7.866%. On that day, on-the-run 10-year Treasury notes (coupon rate: 6⅞%) were priced at 100²⁵⁄32 to yield 6.77%. Thus, the yield spread of GNMA 7.5s versus the 10-year Treasury was 110 basis points. GNMAs of different coupons are priced differently and have different projected cash flows. Therefore, they have different average lives and yields. Exhibit 5 shows different yield spreads of various coupons of GNMAs versus their respective comparable Treasuries. While there is no credit quality difference between GNMAs and Treasuries, the former offeres the opportunity for considerably more yields than the latter due to the uncertainty of their prepayments.

Exhibit 5: Prices, Yields, and Yield Spreads of Selected Generic 30-Year GNMAs under a Constant PSA Speed, May 30, 1996

Coupon (%)	Price (32nds)	Speed (% PSA)	Yield (%)	Average Life (yrs)	Yield of Comp Treasury (%)	Yield Spread (bps)
6	90-11	100	7.60	10.6	6.78	82
6.5	92-30	115	7.73	10.1	6.77	96
7	95-20	120	7.78	10.3	6.78	100
7.5	98-08	130	7.87	10.0	6.77	110
8	100-20	180	7.96	8.4	6.75	121
8.5	102-20	300	7.90	5.6	6.62	128
9	104-17	350	7.67	4.4	6.50	117
9.5	106-23	400	7.22	3.7	6.42	80

Source: Oppenheimer & Co., Inc.

DURATION

As stated at the beginning of this chapter, the market price of a fixed income security is a ratio of the present value of its cash flow to its original principal balance. Since the principal balance is given, the price of the security is inversely associated with its yield (the discount rate for the present value). Thus, as yield rises, the price of the security declines, and vice versa. The sensitivity of the price in response to the change in yield is measured by duration.

Macaulay Duration

For a fixed income security, Macaulay duration is the present-value weighted average time to receive its cash flow. Exhibit 3 shows that at a price of 98⁸⁄₃₂, the Macaulay duration of GNMA 7.5s is 6.11. It is derived from the following formula:

$$\text{Macaulay Duration} = (1/12) \times \{[(1 \times CF_1 / (1 + Y/12)^{1-1+d/30}$$
$$+ 2 \times CF_2 / (1 + Y/12)^{2-1+d/30} + ... + N \times CF_N /(1 + Y/12)^{N-1+d/30}]\}$$
$$/ \{[(CF_1 / (1 + Y/12)^{1-1+d/30} + CF_2 / (1 + Y/12)^{2-1+d/30} + ...$$
$$+ CF_N /(1 + Y/12)^{N-1+d/30}]\}$$

where

CF_N	=	cash flow of period N
Y	=	annual mortgage yield of mortgage pass-through
d	=	actual payment delay, which for GNMAs is 14 days
N	=	month elapsed from settlement date to the actual receipt of principal and interest, which goes from 1, 2, ..., to N (in the present case, $N = 355$)

The denominator of the above equation is actually the present value of the security's future cash flow. Therefore, the Macaulay duration equation can be simplified and rewritten as:

$$\text{Macaulay Duration} = [1/12 \times PV] \times \{[(1 \times CF_1 / (1 + Y/12)^{1-1+d/30} + 2$$
$$\times CF_2 / (1 + Y/12)^{2-1+d/30} + ... + N \times CF_N / (1 + Y/12)^{N-1+d/30}]\}$$

Again, by applying the cash flow in Exhibit 1, the Macaulay duration of GNMA 7.5s is

$$\text{Macaulay Duration} = [1/(12 \times 98250)] \times \{[(1 \times 825.45 / (1 + 0.0774/12)^{1-1+44/30}$$
$$+ 2 \times 846.25 / (1 + 0.0774/12)^{2-1+44/30} + ...$$
$$+ 355 \times 71.84/ (1 + 0.0774/12)^{355-1+44/30}]\}$$
$$= [1/(12 \times 98250)] \times \{817.70 + 1665.88 + ... + 2594.46\}$$
$$= [1/(12 \times 98250)] \times \{7222208.14\}$$
$$= 6.13$$

It is important to note that the duration computation includes the entire cash flow of the security, principal and interest. The average life calculation, however, includes only the principal portion of the cash flow.

Modified Duration

Modified duration measures the sensitivity of the price of a fixed income security in response to changes in its yield. The modified duration is derived by adjusting the Macaulay duration by a factor of $(1 + BEY/2)$. That is:

$$\text{Modified Duration} = \text{Macaulay Duration} / (1 + BEY / 2)$$
$$= 6.13 / (1 + 0.07866 / 2) = 5.89$$

As a convenience, modified duration can be approximated by a simplified formula:

$$\text{Modified Duration} = 100 \times \{(P_H - P_L) / [(Y_L - Y_H) \times P]\}$$

where

P = the initial price before the change in yield
P_H = the price associated with the higher yield
P_L = the price associated with the lower yield
Y_H = a higher bond equivalent yield
Y_L = a lower bond equivalent yield

Thus, at a price of 98 8/32 and a 130% PSA, the bond equivalent yield of GNMA 7.5s is 7.866%. If the bond equivalent yield declines to 6.866% at a 130% PSA, the price of GNMA 7.5s would rise to 104.375. (This calculation is easily done with the Quick Yield Analysis on Bloomberg by simply changing the bond equivalent to 6.866%.) Conversely, if yield rises to 8.866%, the corresponding price is 92.75. Therefore, the modified duration of GNMA 7.5s is

$$100 \times (92.75 - 104.375) / [(6.866 - 8.866) \times 98.25] = 5.91$$

This is very close to the 5.89 computed from adjusting the Macaulay duration. It is important to note that this duration (listed under "static prepayment assumption" of Exhibit 2) assumes a constant prepayment speed. That is, the prepayment assumption for the projected cash flow remains unchanged at a 130% PSA, despite the changing yield.

Effective Duration

Mortgage pass-throughs are unique fixed income securities because of their cash flow uncertainty due to prepayments. In fact, one thing that is certain of mortgage securities is that as yields (commonly represented by market interest rates) change, their prepayments will also change. But the changing interest rates will alter future cash flows of mortgage pass-throughs. Thus, to be realistic in estimating the "effective duration" for a given change in the yield of a mortgage pass-through, the resulting change in its price should take a different prepayment pattern into consideration. Thus, the formula of modified duration should be "further modified" as follows:

$$\text{Effective Duration} = 100 \times \{(P_{L,F} - P_{H,S}) / [(Y_H - Y_L) \times P]\}$$

where

P = the initial price before the change in yield
$P_{L,F}$ = the price associated with a lower yield and a faster speed
$P_{H,S}$ = the price associated with a higher yield and a slower speed

For example, if interest rates decline, GNMA 7.5s are expected to experience acceleration of prepayment. For a 100 basis point decline in yield, their price rise on an accelerated speed of 280% PSA. The new price is 102.8854 (Exhibit 2), markedly lower than that under a 130% PSA. This is primarily because investors become less enthusiastic to purchase pass-throughs at above par prices when prepayments are accelerating. Conversely, in a rising interest rate environment, prepayments are expected to drop. For a 100 basis point increase in yield, GNMA 7.5s are expected to prepay at a 110% PSA. The price corresponding to this prepayment assumption is 92.3255, modestly lower than under a 130% PSA. As prepayments drop, the expected average life of GNMA 7.5s lengthens. For a longer average life, the corresponding price has to decline more significantly. The effective duration of GNMA 7.5s in this scenario is

$$100 \times (102.8854 - 92.3255) / [(6.866 - 8.866) \times 98.25] = 5.36$$

This value is significantly less than the modified duration of 5.89. The smaller effective duration suggests that when prepayments are taken into consideration, the sensitivity of prices of mortgage pass-throughs to changing yields is markedly reduced.

CONVEXITY

Just as duration measures the sensitivity of a security's price to its changing yield, convexity measures the sensitivity of duration to the changing yield. The duration of a security can be long or short, but it is almost always positive.[1] Convexity can be either positive or negative. A security is said to have positive convexity if its

---

[1] The positive duration actually describes the inverse relationship between a security's price and its yield. As will be discussed in a later section, stripped interest-only mortgage securities, or "IOs," have negative duration, meaning that their prices and yields vary in the same direction.

duration becomes increasingly sensitive to continuous changes in yield. If the duration becomes increasingly insensitive, the convexity is negative. Conventionally, it is measured by the following formula:

$$\text{Convexity} = \{[(P_{L,F} - P) / (Y_L - Y) - (P - P_{H,S}) / (Y - Y_H)] / (Y_L - Y_H)\} \times (200 / P)$$

Again, applying the example of GNMA 7.5s, the formula is rewritten as

$$\begin{aligned}\text{Convexity} = \{&[(102.8854 - 98.25) / (6.866 - 7.866) \\ &- (98.25 - 92.3255) / (7.866 - 8.866)] / (6.866 - 8.866)\} \\ &\times (200 / 98.25) = -1.31\end{aligned}$$

The negative convexity of GNMA 7.5s indicates that as yield changes continuously, their duration becomes increasingly shorter. In layman's terms, convexity can be viewed as a security's upside potential versus the downside risk in a continuous change in yield. As demonstrated in the duration analysis, the price of GNMA 7.5s rises less when its yield declines relative to the price decline when yield rises. It reflects that the upside potential of price appreciation of GNMA 7.5s when yield declines is less than the downside depreciation when yield rises. Therefore, they have negative convexity. In fact, it is not just GNMA 7.5s that have negative convexity. With the rare exception of deeply discounted coupons, almost all mortgage pass-throughs have negative convexity. It varies only by degree.

OPTION ADJUSTED ANALYSIS

Thus far, the calculations of yield, yield spread, duration, and convexity of a mortgage pass-through are based on an assumption of a constant prepayment rate for the security. These calculations could be misleading because they do not take into consideration the potential variations of future interest rates and the resulting changes in prepayments of the mortgage security. One popular way of addressing the shortcoming of the above calculations is to conduct an *option adjusted analysis*. For a pass-through, the analysis produces option adjusted spread (OAS), option adjusted duration (OAD), and option adjusted convexity (OAC) under a wide range of interest rate and prepayment scenarios. Based on the wide range of scenarios, the option adjusted analysis provides an objective way of evaluating mortgage securities.

The option adjusted analysis has two major components: simulation of interest rates and projection of prepayments. The most important result of the analysis is the OAS. It is obtained in the following three steps:

Simulation of Interest Rates

There are many ways to simulate interest rates. A popular one, however, is the Monte Carlo method. It randomly generates numerous time-dependent interest rate paths. Simulated interest rate paths are to have a log-normal distribution such that their average is equal to the implied forward path based on the current shape of the Treasury yield curve and their standard deviation is consistent with the assumed interest rate volatility. (Generally, the volatility is assumed to be between 13% and 18%.) The implied forward path is based on the term structure of zero-coupon Treasury yields, which are derived from on-the-run Treasury yields.

The simulation has an internal adjustment such that all Treasuries under simulated paths have an identical expected return. While thousands of interest rate paths may be generated to closely estimate the OAS, they can be limited to as few as 200. Through a variance reduction method, the statistical properties of the 200 paths are set to be internally consistent with those of a larger number of paths. Based on simulated interest rates, 30-year fixed mortgage rates are derived from the 10-year Treasury yield assuming a constant spread between the two.

Projection of Prepayments

Based on derived mortgage rates, the monthly principal paydown for the remaining maturity of a mortgage security is projected. The projection is based on a prepayment model. As mentioned in Chapter 4, the prepayment model is usually a multiple regression equation with at least five explanatory variables:

> *1. The ramp period.* The PSA ramp is the time period for a mortgage pool to reach a mature stage, where prepayments will not continue to escalate through aging. A normal PSA ramp lasts 30 months. However, it is widely believed that in substantially low mortgage rates, the PSA ramp will become markedly shorter than 30 months. Conversely, in an exceedingly high interest rate environment, the ramp period can be much longer than 30 months. Also, 15-year securities are believed to have a shorter PSA ramp than 30-year securities.

> *2. The refinancing incentive.* In declining mortgage rate scenarios, the refinancing incentive measures the magnitude of additional prepayments beyond the core prepayment rate due to housing turnover. In rising mortgage rates, however, the refinancing is nonexistent. Also, in a substantial declining rate environment, 30-year securities have a greater refinancing incentive than 15-year securities, and vice versa. This is because the refinancing of a 30-year debt entails a far greater savings of interest payment than a 15-year debt. Conversely, in a substantial rising rate environment, a 30-year debt is more valuable and the mortgagor will hold onto it longer than a 15-year debt.

> *3. The burnout factor.* Empirically, it has been evident that the refinancing incentive diminishes as the mortgage pool undergoes cycles of declining rates and more interest rate-sensitive mortgagors prepay. The burnout fac-

tor captures this phenomenon. Through this factor, the prepayment model can approximate the burnout speed of a mortgage security when its remaining balance is depleted by refinancing to just a small portion of the original balance.

4. *The seasonal factor.* The seasonal factor reflects the fluctuation of housing activity during a year. It is applied only to the core prepayment rate. This factor adjusts monthly prepayments downward in fall and winter, and upward in spring and summer.

5. *The time lag.* There is normally a one- to two-month lag between the time mortgage rates change and the resulting change in prepayments. Prepayment models usually estimate the time lag in their projections of short-term prepayments.

Calculation of OAS

For each interest rate path, the present value (theoretical price) of the corresponding monthly cash flow of coupon interest and principal paydown of the mortgage security is calculated. For each monthly cash flow, the corresponding discount rate is set to equal to a zero-coupon Treasury yield plus a spread. Since the zero-coupon Treasury yield is already simulated, the spread is derived through an iterative process such that the average of the numerous theoretical prices is equal to the market price of the mortgage security. The derived spread is the option adjusted spread. The computed OAS for a mortgage security is no longer a spread over the comparable average-life Treasury (one spot of the yield curve), but rather a spread over the entire zero-coupon Treasury yield curve. The OAS analysis measures objectively the relative value of a mortgage security because it nets out the option cost that is embedded in the security. The comparison of OASs of mortgage securities with different coupon and maturity characteristics — under identical assumptions of interest rate volatility — therefore reveals objectively the relative value of the individual mortgage securities.

Applications

In addition to the computation of OAS for various mortgage securities (see Exhibit 6 as an example), the OAS model has two important applications: interest rate risk hedging and horizon analysis.

For interest rate hedging, the OAS model produces option adjusted duration (OAD) and option adjusted convexity (OAC). OAD measures the expected percentage change in the option adjusted price of a mortgage security given a marginal change in interest rates and the resulting change in prepayments. This objective measurement differs from the traditional one-dimensional modified duration which treats the price of a mortgage security simply as a function of interest rates regardless of the relationship between interest rates and prepayments. However, it is close to the effective duration. For example, the OAD of 30-year GNMA 7.5s, according to Exhibit 6, is 5.4. Its effective duration in Exhibit 3 is 5.36. Conceptually, effective convexity is consistent to effective duration. It measures the upside or downside potential of a mortgage security given a continued change in interest rates.

Based on the objectivity of the OAS analysis, the horizon analysis — total return of a mortgage for a given holding period — can be analyzed. As will be discussed in Chapter 10, there are four components in a holding-period return: change in price at the end of the holding period, interim prepayment, coupon income, and reinvestment of coupon interest and principal paydown. Among the four, end-period prices are the most critical. By assuming a constant OAS under various interest rate scenarios, the OAS model can compute the end-period prices of the mortgage security. The OAS-constant total return is superior to the conventional constant-yield-spread total return analysis because it factors in the impact of changing interest rates on the future cash flow of the mortgage security not just for the holding period but for the remaining maturity of the security.

Exhibit 6: Option Adjusted Analysis of Selected New Production
Generic 30-Year GNMAs, May 30, 1996

Coupon (%)	Price (32nds)	Static Spread (bp)	OAS (bp)	OAD	OAC
6	90-11	73	57	6.6	0.3
6.5	92-30	88	65	6.3	0.0
7	95-20	99	67	6.0	−0.3
7.5	98-08	111	70	5.4	−0.6
8	100-20	124	72	4.9	−0.8
8.5	102-20	133	75	4.1	−1.1
9	104-17	107	60	3.0	−0.9
9.5	106-23	48	20	2.2	−0.5

Note: Static and option adjusted spreads are computed assuming 0% and 13% volatility, respectively.
Source: Oppenheimer & Co., Inc.

Chapter 6

Adjustable-Rate Mortgages and Mortgage Pass-Throughs

- Historical Perspective of the Primary ARM Market
- ARM Indexes
- Other Features of ARMs
- ARM Pass-Throughs
- Prepayments of ARM Pass-Throughs
- Pricing and Evaluation of ARM Pass-Throughs
- Current Trading of Agency ARM Pass-Throughs

HISTORICAL PERSPECTIVE OF THE PRIMARY ARM MARKET

While adjustable-rate mortgages (ARMs) have existed since the late 1970s, they only began to become an important housing finance instrument in 1983. Historically high rates on fixed-rate mortgages (FRMs) in the early 1980s and aggressive marketing by thrift institutions made ARMs popular among home buyers. A review of the growth of ARMs between 1984 and 1996 reveals that the origination share of ARMs was positively influenced by the FRM-ARM rate differential when FRM rates exceeded 10%. But as FRM rates dropped to single digits — particularly below 8%, as was the case in 1993 and 1995 — FRMs dominated the origination market, regardless of the FRM-ARM rate differential.

Alternative Housing Finance Instrument

In the early 1980s, when FRM rates were prohibitively high, in excess of 18%, ARMs were timely and attractive alternatives to FRMs. Although they plunged more than 400 basis points in 1982, FRM rates were still too high to qualify many buyers for home purchases (Exhibit 1). ARMs, which became increasingly available with initial rates much below FRM rates, proved to be popular among home buyers. (Information on monthly ARM rates became available only in 1984. However, anecdotal evidence indicated that, prior to 1984, ARMs were offered at initial rates at least 200 basis points below FRM rates.) In 1983, originations of ARMs amounted to $75 billion, accounting for almost 40% of the total market. The popularity of ARMs in 1983 also helped the housing market to recover from the deep 1980-82 recession. During the dozen years that followed, annual ARM originations amounted to at least $120 billion and accounted for between 20% and 60% of the market (Exhibit 2).

Exhibit 1: Monthly Fixed and Adjustable Mortgage Rates, and Fixed-Adjustable Rate Spread, 1/80 to 6/96

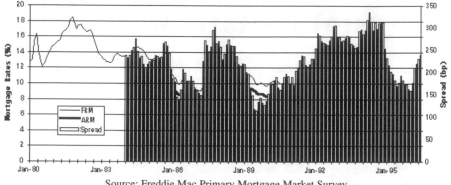

Source: Freddie Mac Primary Mortgage Market Survey

Exhibit 2: Annual 1-4 Family Mortgage Originations by Mortgage Type and ARM Market Share, 1983-1996*

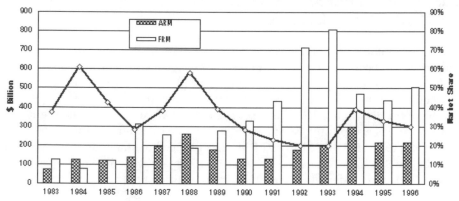

* Figures for 1996 are annualized based on six-month data.
Sources: U.S. Department of Housing and Urban Development and Federal Housing Finance Board

Aggressive Marketing by Thrifts

ARMs owed their initial popularity to aggressive marketing by thrift institutions. The powerful bond market rally of 1982 pulled thrifts from the verge of bankruptcy. But as thrifts regained their financial health, pressure was mounting for them to reduce the maturity mismatch of their assets and liabilities. While ARMs had the same maturities as FRMs (25 to 30 years), the adjustable-rate feature brought the funding frequency much closer to the maturities of the thrifts' liabilities. Thus, originating ARMs was an important balance sheet strategy for thrifts. They aggressively marketed ARMs to home buyers and became major ARM originators.

Exhibit 3: Monthly Rate Spread between FRMs and ARMs and ARM Market Share, 1/84 to 6/96

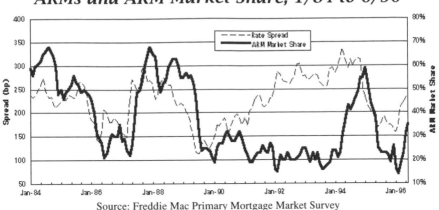

Source: Freddie Mac Primary Mortgage Market Survey

Two-Tier Relationship between FRMs and ARMs

The history of ARM originations in the January 1984 - June 1996 period reveals a two-tier relationship between ARMs and FRMs. When FRM rates were 10% or higher, the origination share of ARMs associated positively with both the absolute level of FRMs and the FRM-ARM rate differential. This relationship existed during the housing expansion between 1984 and 1990. As shown in Exhibit 3, the monthly origination share of ARMs fluctuated in this seven-year period between a little under 20% and 70%. The fluctuation was basically the result of home buyers reacting to the oscillating FRM rates. In particular, in 1984 and 1988, when FRM rates were rising and the FRM-ARM rate differential hovered mostly above 250 basis points, ARMs accounted for as much as 65% of total originations. In 1986, however, as FRM rates were declining with the FRM-ARM rate differential shrinking below 200 basis points, the market share of ARMs dropped mostly under 30%.

Between 1991 and 1996, however, as FRM rates ranged between 9.7% and the 25-year low of 6.8%, the origination share of ARMs plummeted to as low as 16%. When FRM rates were below 9%, the origination market share of ARMs became a sole function of the level of FRM rates — the lower the FRM rates, the smaller the ARM market share became, regardless of their rate differential. This simplified one-dimensional relationship reflected that when FRM rates were historically low, home buyers overwhelmingly preferred FRMs to ARMs.

ARM INDEXES

In their early stage, ARMs were indexed primarily to the cost of funds of thrifts or FRM rates. Understandably, thrifts were major ARM originators and preferred ARM indexes that either reflected the market interest rates of their liabilities or floated with market FRM rates. Three indexes were common then: the National Median Cost of Funds Index (the national COFI), the Eleventh District Cost of Funds Index (the 11th COFI, or simply COFI because of its wide popularity among thrifts on the West Coast), and the national average mortgage contract rate on closed loans for the purchase of existing homes (the Mortgage Contract Rate).

As ARMs gradually established themselves as a viable alternative to FRMs, both as a housing finance instrument as well as an investment vehicle, their indexes proliferated. The new indexes included: the six-month, one-, three-, and five-year constant maturity Treasuries (CMTs), the six-month LIBOR, and the six-month rate on certificates of deposit (CDs). In recent years, however, the choice of index has narrowed. The majority of ARMs now rely on three indexes: the COFI, the six-month LIBOR, and the one-year CMT (Exhibit 4). In general, the six-month LIBOR and the one-year CMT respond to market conditions much more quickly than COFI does, both in upward and downward directions. The six-month LIBOR and the one-year CMT therefore are far more volatile than COFI.

COFI

COFI represents the annualized weighted average interest on all sources of funds paid monthly by member savings institutions located in the Eleventh District of the Federal Home Loan Bank System (FHLB). These institutions are insured by the Savings Associations Insurance Fund. The Eleventh District, with headquarters in San Francisco, covers Arizona, California, and Nevada. However, California has consistently accounted for over 90% of member institutions in the Eleventh District. The San Francisco FHLB calculates and publishes COFI on a monthly basis. There are three sources of funds for COFI: deposits, FHLB advances, and other borrowings. Deposits have always been the most important source of funds, followed by advances and other borrowings.

Exhibit 4: COFI, the Six-Month LIBOR, and the One-Year CMT, 1/82 to 6/96

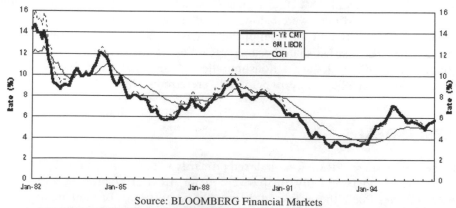

Source: BLOOMBERG Financial Markets

Exhibit 5: Volatility of the COFI, the SIx-Month LIBOR and the One-Year CMT, 1/83 to 6/96

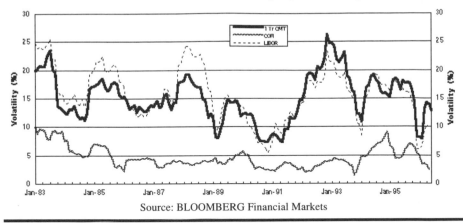

Source: BLOOMBERG Financial Markets

The Six-Month LIBOR

The London Interbank Offered Rates on Eurodollar deposits traded between banks is referred to as LIBOR. There are different rates on the deposits depending on their maturities. The rate on six-month Eurodollar deposits is the six-month LIBOR. It is an average of quoted rates from 16 banks. On a daily basis (11 a.m. London time), the British Bankers' Association computes the average of only the middle eight quotes and determines the daily six-month LIBOR.

The One-Year CMT

The yield on the one-year CMT is interpolated from the daily Treasury yield curve. It covers the yields of all outstanding Treasury securities, regardless of original maturities, with a remaining maturity of one year. The Federal Reserve Bank of New York gathers daily the one-year yield quotes from five leading U.S. government securities dealers and computes their average as the one-year CMT. The Board of Governors of the Federal Reserve System publishes each Monday the weekly average of daily one-year CMTs through the Federal Reserve Statistical Release, Series H-15.

The Volatility of COFI versus the Six-Month LIBOR and the One-Year CMT

Volatility is measured here as the annualized standard deviation of the monthly percent change of the index over the past 12 months. Since COFI is an index that represents the weighted average interest paid on numerous liabilities of various maturities, it does not move as quickly as the one-year CMT or the six-month LIBOR in response to the daily change in market conditions. Also, COFI is calculated on a monthly basis and weighted by the month-end balance of liabilities. It cannot reflect the short-term fluctuation of money market conditions during the month. For these reasons, as shown in Exhibit 5, the volatility of COFI is low, hovering mostly between 3% and 6%. By comparison, the volatility of the one-year CMT and the six-month LIBOR ranges mostly between 10% and 20%.

OTHER FEATURES OF ARMS

In addition to the selection of an index for the interest-rate adjustment, ARMs differ from one another with respect to other features such as interest rate reset period, gross margin, initial rate, caps for interest rate or payment adjustment, and convertibility to fixed-rate mortgages.

Interest Rate Reset Period

The *reset period*, or *term of adjustment*, is the frequency of adjustment in the note rate of the ARM. Originally, the reset period varied from one month to five years. In recent years, however, the reset period has been mostly six months or one year. Nevertheless, some COFI-indexed ARMs (COFI ARMs) still retain the monthly rate reset feature. But the monthly payment is usually adjusted only once a year to protect borrowers from frequent and drastic upward adjustment in the mortgage note rate.

Gross Margin

The *gross margin* is the interest rate spread that is added to the index rate at the reset to determine the new mortgage note rate. Depending on the index, the gross margin varies mostly between 150 and 300 basis points. This margin is termed "gross" to differentiate from the "net margin" of ARM pass-throughs. For the coupon rate of pass-throughs, the cost of servicing is subtracted from the gross margin to arrive at the net margin.

Mortgage Note Rate

The mortgage note rate is the sum of the index rate and the gross margin.

Initial Rate

ARMs are often offered at an initial rate that is substantially below the mortgage note rate. This low initial rate is often referred to as the "teaser rate."

Rate Caps

To protect borrowers from "rate-adjustment shock," most ARMs have a limitation on the periodic adjustment (the *periodic cap*). On a cumulative basis, ARMs also have a limitation on rate adjustment for the life of the mortgage (the *lifetime cap*). The periodic cap is usually 100 to 200 basis points on an annualized basis. The lifetime cap is typically 500 to 600 basis points above the initial rate. Colloquially, an ARM with a "2/6 cap" refers to a 200 basis point annualized cap and a 600 basis point lifetime cap.

Monthly Payment Caps

To the extent that ARMs have no rate caps, they have instead a monthly payment cap. Again, this is to protect borrowers from too sharp an upward adjustment in the note rate. The most popular payment cap limits the annualized increase in the monthly payment to 7.5%. Any shortfall between the 7.5% payment increase and the necessary increase to amortize the mortgage will be added on to the mortgage's remaining balance. This process is called *negative amortization*, since the remaining balance increases rather than decreases as in a normal amortization. COFI ARMs sometimes have negative amortization because they allow monthly reset of the note rate but only annual adjustment in the monthly payment. Most one-year CMT and LIBOR ARMs do not have negative amortization, as they only have rate caps.

Convertibility to Fixed-Rate Mortgages

To enhance the marketing of ARMs, lenders sometimes offer borrowers the option of converting the adjustable-rate feature to fixed-rate after the first year. This option, which usually lasts for up to five years, is particularly attractive to home-owners during periods of declining interest rates. Not only do the borrowers benefit from the decline in rates during the adjustment period, they also can lock in the lower rate permanently through conversion.

ARM PASS-THROUGHS

As ARMs have become a viable alternative housing finance instrument for home buyers, ARM-backed pass-throughs have been increasingly accepted by investors as attractive investments. As shown in Exhibit 6, only 2% of ARM originations were securitized in 1983. By contrast, 65% of FRMs were already pooled for the issuance of pass-throughs. But securitization of ARMs expanded steadily in the following 10 years. By 1993, 38% of ARM originations were pooled for pass-throughs, more than half of the securitization ratio of FRMs. In 1994 and 1995, however, the securitization ratio of ARMs dropped to around 25%. All agencies — particularly GNMA in recent years — have been active in securitizing ARMs.

GNMA ARMs

While GNMA initiated its ARM securitization program early in 1983, the annual issuance of GNMA ARMs never exceeded $3 billion until 1991 (Exhibit 7). One reason for the consistently meager volume was the relatively rigid structure of the FHA/VA ARMs, which are pooled for GNMAs. (Because of the expiration of the VA ARM Program, current GNMA ARMs are backed exclusively by FHA ARMs.) They are indexed only to the one-year CMT. More important, GNMA ARMs have a limited 100 basis point annual interest rate cap and a 500 basis point lifetime cap. Initially, investors were reluctant to purchase adjustable-rate securities whose annual rate adjustment was limited to just one percentage point.

Exhibit 6: Annual Issuance of Pass-Throughs as a Percentage of Newly Originated Mortgages, 1983 to 1996*

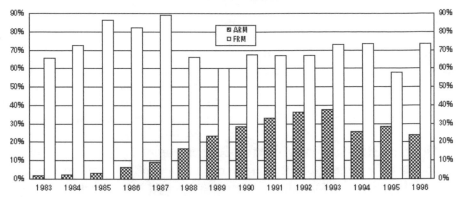

* Figures for 1996 are annualized based on six-month data.
Source: Inside Mortgage Securities

Exhibit 7: Annual Issuance of ARM Pass-Throughs by Guarantor, 1983 to 1996*

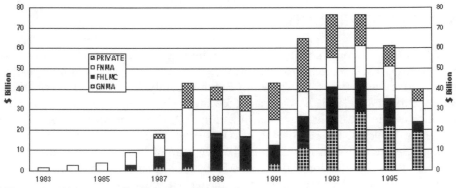

* Figures for 1996 are annualized based on six-month data.
Source: Inside Mortgage Securities

However, the issuance of GNMA ARMs soared to $11 billion in 1992 and nearly tripled that amount to $29 billion in 1994 before falling off moderately to $23 billion in 1995. The sudden popularity of GNMA ARMs is attributable to the rapidly declining interest rates and persistently flat yield curve during these two years. To investors, the 100 basis point annual cap was no longer a "limited cap" in a period when interest rates hovered around historically low levels with long-term rates not much higher than short-term rates. To FHA/VA borrowers, who are mostly low and moderate income home buyers, historically low initial rates in the neighborhood of 4% to 5% were particularly attractive.

GNMA ARMs are issued under the GNMA II Program. Thus, they are backed by multiple-issuer pools, and the underlying mortgage note rates can differ up to 100 basis points. These mortgages have a gross margin ranging between 150 and 300 basis points, although the most popular margin is 200 basis points. With a 50 basis point servicing fee, the popular *net margin* for GNMA ARMs is 150 basis points.

All underlying mortgages of GNMA ARMs have the same interest reset date. They are synchronized to one of the following four dates: the first day of April, July, October, and January. The reset of the new coupon rate is calculated by adding the net margin to the index rate 30 days before the adjustment date and rounding the sum to the nearest ⅛%. The index rate is determined by the weekly average yield of one-year constant maturity Treasury notes published by the Board of Governors of Federal Reserve System.

FNMA ARMs

FNMA also commenced its ARM securities programs in 1983, although the issuance volume in that year was a modest $1.4 billion. By 1988, however, annual issuance of FNMA ARMs had expanded to $21.6 billion. Between 1989 and 1995, it ranged between $12 and $18 billion, averaging $14.2 billion. In the early years, the bulk of FNMA ARMs were indexed to COFI with a net margin of 125 basis points and a one- or six-month interest-rate reset period. Recently, however, the issuance of COFI ARMs has declined markedly. Changes in accounting rules and regulations for financial institutions have directed thrifts to originate COFI ARMs for their own portfolios rather than for sale in the form of pass-throughs. Consequently, FNMA ARMs have switched primarily to the one-year CMT with a small portion indexed to the six-month LIBOR. The net margins of the one-year CMT and the six-month LIBOR are around 175 to 240 and 150 to 225 basis points, respectively. The one-year CMT ARMs generally have a 200 basis point annual cap; and the six-month LIBOR ARMs, a 100 basis point semi-annual cap. Both have a 500 to 600 basis point life-time cap.

FHLMC ARMs

Although FHLMC started its ARM securities program late in 1986, issuance of FHLMC ARMs quickly reached $7.3 billion in 1988. Between 1989 and 1995, annual issuance of FHLMC ARMs ranged between $9 and $21 billion, averaging $15.7 billion. They were mostly indexed to the one-year CMT. In recent years, their net margins have been around 200 to 240 basis points. A smaller portion of FHLMC ARMs are also indexed to the six-month LIBOR with a net margin of 225 to 250 basis points.

Private-Label ARMs

Adjustable-rate mortgage loans whose original balances exceed the FNMA/FHLMC mortgage securities program limits are pooled for private-label pass-throughs. As will be mentioned in Chapter 8, credit enhancements for these securities include senior/subordinate structure, corporate parent guarantees, mortgage pool insurance policies, and commercial bank letters of credit. In recent years, the senior/subordinate structure has been the most popular form of credit enhancement and the credit of private-label ARMs has been mostly AAA- or AA-rated. There is no comprehensive data source tabulating the various features of private-label ARMs, but they are believed to be indexed mostly to the one-year CMT and the six-month LIBOR with net margins similar to those of FNMA/FHLMC ARMs.

PREPAYMENTS OF ARM PASS-THROUGHS

Determinants of Prepayments
The factors that influence prepayments of ARM pass-throughs are similar to those of FRM pass-throughs. They include: the level of the prevailing FRM rates, the spread between the coupon rate and the market rate, the seasonality of the housing market, the age of the mortgage pool, the shape of the yield curve, and the availability of other competitive mortgages. The last two determinants are particularly important to ARM pass-throughs. When the yield curve turns steeper, ARMs are more likely to be refinanced than FRMs. Also, ARMs are more likely to be refinanced into other ARMs with lower teaser rates. For these reasons, ARM pass-throughs tend to have a higher prepayment rate with a tighter range among the various coupons than FRM pass-throughs.

FNMA/FHLMC Prepayments
Current production FNMA/FHLMC ARMs are usually priced with a prepayment rate of 15% to 18% CPR, while FRM pass-throughs are priced with 6% to 9% CPR. (Since there is no established pattern of what constitutes seasoned pools for ARM pass-throughs, their prepayments are measured in CPR rather than in PSA, as is the case of FRM pass-throughs.) Convertible ARMs are usually priced at 18% to 20% CPR; non-convertibles, around 15% CPR. Premium-coupon ARM pass-throughs have rarely prepaid at more than 40% CPR as FRM pass-throughs did during the refinancing boom of the past two years. Conversely, discount-coupon ARMs seldom experienced prepayment speeds slower than 10% CPR as FRM pass-throughs did during periods of high interest rates such as the late-1980s.

GNMA ARM Prepayments
Like their FRM counterparts, GNMA ARMs have a much slower prepayment rate than FNMA/FHLMC ARMs. For one thing, GNMA ARMs are indexed exclusively to the one-year CMT with no option to convert to fixed-rate. Further, FHA/VA ARMs with their low initial rates have limited alternatives to refinance. Besides, they are assumable, which further depresses prepayments. A FHA/VA financed home can be sold with the buyer assuming the mortgage. Current-coupon GNMA ARMs are usually priced at 8% to 10% CPR.

Despite their 10-year history, it is difficult to construct prepayment models of ARM pass-throughs with the same sophistication as those of FRM pass-throughs. Most important, it was only since 1991 that the outstanding volume of ARM pass-throughs became significant enough to produce consistent data for statistical analysis of prepayments. Even during this period, prepayment data was sketchy because of the wide variety of ARMs in terms of the index, the reset period, the interest rate cap, and the net margin.

PRICING AND EVALUATION OF ARM PASS-THROUGHS

The DM and the BEEM

Like any fixed-income security, the price of an ARM pass-through is the present value of its future cash flow based on an assumed constant prepayment rate. The discount rate of the cash flow is its yield, which is the sum of a spread called the *discount margin* (*DM*) and the index rate. Since the ARM pass-through pays monthly, the discount margin is derived on monthly compounding.

In order to compare the DM to the yield spread of semi-annual-pay securities, the cash flow yield of the ARM pass-through is converted to a bond-equivalent basis. The spread between the bond-equivalent cash flow yield of the ARM pass-through and its index rate is the *bond-equivalent effective margin* (*BEEM*). The BEEM is always higher than the DM. As pointed out in Chapter 5, the difference between the mortgage yield (DM) and the bond-equivalent yield (BEEM) is the "add-on." For a 6% to 8% mortgage yield, the add-on ranges between 8 and 14 basis points.

Although the BEEM is derived assuming unchanged interest rates, it is a useful yardstick for evaluating the various features of ARM pass-throughs. For example, a brand new non-convertible Conventional (FNMA or FHLMC) ARM indexed to the one-year CMT with a 225 basis point net margin (gross margin: 300 basis points), with an annual reset, a 2/6 cap, and a 6% coupon is priced at 101. Assuming an 18% CPR, this security has a bond-equivalent cash flow yield of 7.38%. At the current index rate of 5.82%, this security has a BEEM of 156 basis points (7.38% – 5.82%).

Since the coupon rate of this security is 207 basis points below the fully indexed rate (5.82% + 225 basis points – 6%), it is a "teaser" ARM. In this case, the reset frequency and the annual/lifetime caps are important variables that can affect the size of the BEEM. For example, other things being constant, if the reset period is shortened to six months (the periodic cap is now 100 basis points), the BEEM of this pass-through at the same price will rise 12 basis points to 168. A quarterly reset (period cap: 50 basis points) raises the BEEM further to 174 basis points. The incremental effective margin reflects the value of the reset frequency. Even though interest rates are assumed to remain unchanged, the more frequent the interest-rate reset, the sooner the coupon rate can be adjusted closer to the fully indexed rate. This enhances the value of the security.

On the other hand, holding other things constant, if the size of the annual cap is enlarged to 300 basis points, the BEEM will be 1 basis point wider at 157 basis points. Conversely, if the annual cap is limited to 100 basis points, the BEEM will shrink by 18 basis points to 138. This indicates that a 200 basis point annual cap is already generous enough to allow upward adjustment in mortgage rates. Consequently, enlarging the cap will add little value to the ARM pass-through. However, a 100 basis point cap is too restrictive for the rate adjustment. It makes the pass-through rather unattractive.

The Option-Adjusted Spread

In reality, as interest rates change, the BEEM cannot always capture the impact of changing interest rates on the reset frequency and caps. More important, ARMs with different indexes cannot be readily compared and evaluated by their respective BEEMs. To do so, a benchmark spread — an option-adjusted spread (OAS) over the Treasury yield curve — is needed to place all ARM pass-throughs on a level playing field.

The OAS Calculation Using a one-year CMT ARM pass-through as an example, its OAS calculation consists of the following steps. First, simulate numerous future paths of Treasury yields of varying maturities according to the current shape of the Treasury yield curve and the volatility assumptions. Second, based on the numerous simulated Treasury yields and an ARM prepayment model, project their corresponding monthly payment cash flows (interest, amortized and prepaid principal) of the underlying pool of ARMs. Third, through an iterative process, equate the average present value of all cash flows to the market price of the ARM pass-through. During the iterative process, the discount rate for the present value calculation is the sum of the simulated Treasury yield curve plus a spread. This spread is the OAS. (A more detailed discussion of OAS calculation is presented in Chapter 5.)

A Common Yardstick Based on an assumed Treasury-yield volatility, this OAS is the common yardstick to evaluate all ARM pass-throughs and their features. A security with a greater OAS is more attractive than one with a smaller OAS, regardless of their indexes. Moreover, for ARMs of different indexes, the OAS can demonstrate that the reset period and the cap are more valuable to ARMs with a more volatile index. For ARMs of the same index, the OAS can more objectively evaluate the value of the interest-rate reset frequency and the cap than the BEEM.

CURRENT TRADING OF AGENCY ARM PASS-THROUGHS

This section discusses trading characteristics of agency-guaranteed ARM pass-throughs (agency ARMs) indexed to the one-year CMT, the six-month LIBOR, and the COFI. The one-year CMT ARMs are the most important sector of agency ARMs. They have the largest outstanding balance and the greatest trading volume. Within this sector, there are GNMA one-year CMT ARMs and FNMA/FHLMC one-year CMT ARMs. They trade differently, and GNMAs are viewed as the benchmark securities. Both FNMA and FHLMC securitize six-month LIBOR and COFI ARMs. These securities also trade differently depending on the specific features of the underlying mortgage pools.

GNMA ARMs

GNMA ARMs, which are indexed exclusively to the one-year CMT, are the benchmark securities for all ARM pass-throughs. They trade on a to-be-announced (TBA) basis. Their prices are quoted on active inter-dealer broker screens and are regarded as the most important leading indicator of trends in trading of ARM pass-throughs. Additionally, there is an active market for *specified pools of non-TBA eligible* GNMA ARMs. The bid-offer price spread is 2 to 4 ticks for TBAs and 4 to 8 ticks for non-TBAs. There are also *forward trades* of GNMA ARMs generally up to four months.

With their ⅕ annual/life-time caps, GNMA ARM prices are highly sensitive to the levels of Treasury yields. Any important alteration in the overall macroeconomic setting is quickly reflected in GNMA ARM prices and yield spreads. Like FRM pass-throughs, GNMA ARMs trade on a yield spread to the one-year Treasury (the BEEM, as described above). This spread is the most widely used yardstick. Their homogencous characteristics (with regard to synchronized reset frequency, definitive coupons, caps and floors), coupled with the active dealer price screens, make GNMA ARMs unique.

FNMA/FHLMC One-Year CMT ARMs

FNMA/FHLMC one-year CMT ARMs are far less homogeneous and trade on a pool-specific basis. Those with 2/6 caps are most popular, and any divergence from these caps usually results in trading at wider yield spreads. Like other ARMs, the BEEM is the most important indicator of value; others include geographic location of underlying loans, caps and floors, the mortgage-rate dispersion within the given coupon rate of the pool, roll dates and other parameters. Investors typically prefer a more diverse geographic distribution of loans and a lower dispersion of other bond parameters.

The traditional division of ARMs into convertibles and non-convertibles has an important role for FNMA/FHLMC ARMs. Convertibles usually trade a few ticks lower than comparable-coupon non-convertibles. This is due primarily to the greater prepayment risk associated with convertible ARMs. However, in the recent market of relatively stable short-term rates, the prepayment option is perceived to have lost a great deal of its value and the price differential has narrowed. In fact, depending on the prepayment assumption, convertibles and non-convertibles can trade at about the same price.

With the increase in the issuance volume in recent years, an active *TBA forward market* has emerged. For such trades, the index, coupon, margin, reset, and settlement month must be specified before a transaction can take place. The bid-offer spread for FNMA/FHLMC one-year CMT ARMs is 4 to 12 ticks.

FNMA/FHLMC Six-Month LIBOR ARMs
The sector of six-month LIBOR indexed ARMs has grown considerably of late and has emerged as a significant alternative to the traditional one-year CMT ARMs. The LIBOR index has attracted a large number of European and Asian investors. The six-month reset frequency has brought in still more investors, who are attracted by the greater interest rate sensitivity of the index. As a market, six-month LIBOR ARMs trade in a manner similar to one-year CMT ARMs (i.e., investors look at the coupon, margin, caps, floors, and geographic and parameter dispersion). Six-month LIBOR ARMs now trade at about the same bid-offer price spread as one-year CMT ARMs.

FNMA/FHLMC COFI ARMs
Once the most liquid sector of the ARM pass-through market, COFI ARMs have lost much of their luster due to the lack of issuance and the lagging nature of the index. A TBA screen market still exists, but it is fast losing ground. In order to be TBA eligible, securities must be FNMA ARMs with a monthly reset and have a 125 basis point net margin with at least a 12% life-time cap. Equivalent FHLMC ARMs trade $10/32$ to $24/32$ behind their FNMA counterparts. Most monthly COFI ARMs are not convertible, although semi-annual COFI and other more "exotic" COFI index pass-throughs may offer convertible features. COFI ARMs are not attracting much investor interest now because the index rate now is much lower than the one-year CMT and the six-month LIBOR. This situation may change, however, when the COFI bottoms out and begins to catch up with the other indexes. The bid-offer spread for monthly COFI ARMs has widened to 8 to 16 ticks, as the market has lost liquidity. The bid-offer spread for semi-annual reset and other exotic COFI ARMs is now 12 to 24 ticks.

Chapter 7

Multiclass Mortgage Pass-Throughs

- The Need for Multiclass Mortgage Securities
- Collateralized Mortgage Obligations
- Real Estate Mortgage Investment Conduits
- Variety of REMIC Classes
- The Rise and Fall of REMICs
- Prospects for the REMIC Market
- Current Trading of REMICs
- PSA Prepayment Curve Revisited

THE NEED FOR MULTICLASS MORTGAGE SECURITIES

When residential mortgages were first packaged for the issuance of mortgage pass-throughs in 1970, they were securitized as single-class pass-throughs. For accounting and taxation purposes, issuing a pass-through is equivalent to an outright sale of the underlying mortgages. The investor in a pass-through receives a pro rata share of the monthly cash flow generated from the security's underlying pool of mortgages. To avoid taxation at the level of the issuing entity, pass-throughs are issued under a *grantor trust* structure. The significance of this structure is that it requires that the issuer only passively manage the cash flow as a servicer by passing the monthly payment of interest and principal from the underlying mortgagors (less a servicing fee) directly to investors without any interim investing or reallocating of the cash flow. This requirement prohibits the issuer from actively managing the underlying mortgage cash flow. Thus, the pass-through cash flow is legally determined and has a single fixed final maturity date.

While their issuance volume exceeded $100 billion during the first decade of their existence, pass-throughs have inherently undesirable aspects. Their stated final maturity of 30 years is too long for many investors. Worse, their actual maturities and average lives are uncertain. As mentioned in Chapter 4, this uncertainty is caused by the mortgagors' option to prepay at par at any time before maturity without penalties. This prepayment option makes mortgage pass-throughs unattractive to many potential investors.

Mortgagors tend to exercise their prepayment options by refinancing when market mortgage rates decline below their existing rates. However, this is not the environment in which investors want their invested principal prepaid quickly, especially not at par, because the prepaid proceeds can now be reinvested only at lower rates. Conversely, when market rates rise, investors want their invested principal prepaid quickly so that it can be reinvested at higher rates. But, this does not happen. To make matters worse, as rates rise, the housing market inevitably slows down, forcing homeowners to stay put and hold on to their lower-rate mortgages.

The undesirable aspects of long maturity and cash flow uncertainty could be addressed effectively if issuers of mortgage pass-throughs were allowed to actively manage the mortgage cash flow. Under active management, issuers would be able to segment the cash flow in various maturity classes and allocate the prepaid cash flow — and thus the prepayment uncertainty — among these classes. Early prepayment proceeds from the underlying mortgages would go first to retire the shorter maturity classes. As these classes are paid off, prepayments would then retire longer maturity classes.

More important, with the ability to actively manage the cash flow, the issuer can sell the segmented cash flow at different prices according to their expected average lives and maturities. Whereas a single-maturity pass-through is priced at a specified yield on the longer end of the Treasury yield curve, its segmented cash flow could be sold at various yield levels that more closely track the shape of the yield curve. Since the normal shape of the yield curve is positively sloped, a shorter-term cash flow is priced with a lower yield, and therefore a higher price than a longer-term cash flow. By pricing the segmented cash flow along the Treasury yield curve, multiclass securities enhance the value of the underlying mortgages.

COLLATERALIZED MORTGAGE OBLIGATIONS

Despite the obvious market needs, the legal and accounting constraints of the grantor trust arrangement prohibited the issuance of multiclass mortgage pass-throughs. To get around this prohibition, issuers assembled pass-throughs as collateral, segmented their cash flows, and issued collateralized mortgage obligations (CMOs) to satisfy the various maturity demands of investors. As its names implies, a CMO is issued as a debt obligation of the issuer, not an asset sale. As such, it can be in a multiclass format with the issuer actively managing the cash flow of the underlying collateral.

The first CMO was issued by FHLMC in May 1983 for $1 billion. It consisted of three sequential maturity classes with maximum weighted average lives of 3.2 years (Class A-1), 8.6 years (Class A-2), and 20.4 years (Class A-3), respectively. Through semiannual sinking fund payments, Class A-1 was scheduled to be retired before the beginning reduction of the principal balance of Class A-2. Similarly, Class A-3 was not to receive any principal payment until Class A-2 was paid off. Maturity classes created under this type of structure were called *sequentials*. At the pricing date of this first CMO, the 3-, 7-, and 20-year Treasury yields were around 10.3%, 10.6%, and 10.9%, respectively. The three classes were offered at 33, 53, and 90 basis points, respectively, over the 3-, 7-, and 20-year Treasuries. Shorter maturity classes were not only priced at lower yields, but also at tighter yield spreads.

Exhibit 1: Annual Issuance of CMOs and Private-Label REMICs, 1983-1996*

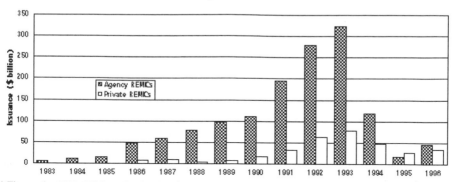

* Figures for 1983-1986 are CMOs; for 1996 are annualized based on six-month data.
Source: Inside Mortgage Securities

CMOs were an instant success, and they revolutionized mortgage-backed securities. In just a little over three years after their debut, total issuance of CMOs approached $80 billion (Exhibit 1). They proved to be far more satisfactory than single-class pass-throughs in matching various investors' maturity preferences. The variety of CMO issuers proliferated to include mortgage bankers, thrifts, home builders, securities dealers, and to a limited extent, banks and insurance companies. Through CMOs, the investor base of mortgage securities greatly expanded. In addition to greater involvement of banks and thrifts, who were the traditional investors, CMOs attracted non-traditional investors such as life insurance companies, pension funds, and foreign investors.

REAL ESTATE MORTGAGE INVESTMENT CONDUITS

Although CMOs were popular among investors, their popularity became a financial burden for their issuers. Since CMOs are issued as debt, not asset sales, their voluminous offerings ballooned their issuers' balance sheets. An increasingly large amount of equity capital was required to support outstanding CMOs. Meanwhile, as the housing market emerged from the recession of the early 1980s, demand for mortgage credit was historically strong. In order for the capital markets to continue to fund the enormous demand for mortgage credit, more new CMOs had to be issued. Therefore, there was tremendous incentive for market participants to persuade Congress to amend the strictures of grantor trust to allow the issuance of multiclass mortgage securities as pass-throughs.

Three years after the creation of CMOs, Congress was finally persuaded to do just that. A provision of the Tax Reform Act of 1986 allowed the issuance of multiclass pass-throughs. It created the real estate mortgage investment conduit

(REMIC), a nontaxable entity in the eyes of the Internal Revenue Service. By electing a REMIC status, issuers can offer multiclass mortgage securities by actively managing the cash flow of the underlying mortgage collateral without any negative tax consequences.

The REMIC legislation furthered the revolution of securitization of residential mortgages. It was the logical next step after the creation of CMOs. The spectacular growth of the REMIC issuance volume speaks for their success. In 1987, when the REMIC legislation became effective, issuance of agency-guaranteed REMICs already approached $80 billion (Exhibit 1). By 1993, issuance of agency REMICs topped $320 billion. (From the structural point of view, there is no appreciable difference between CMOs and REMICs. Although CMOs ceased to exist after 1986, REMICs are still habitually referred to as CMOs.)

The amazing growth, however, came to an abrupt halt in April 1994 due to a unique combination of events that will be discussed later. Since then, for a period of 24 months, issuance of REMICs has averaged only $2.6 billion per month. This rate was less than 10% of the monthly average of 1992-93, the heyday of REMICs. The balance of this chapter will identify a few popular REMIC classes and describe how they trade in the secondary market. It will also explain the rise and fall of the REMIC market and provide a discussion of its future prospects.

VARIETY OF REMIC CLASSES

After the creation of REMICs, not only did the volume of REMIC issuance expand rapidly, but the variety of REMIC classes also proliferated. While at the very beginning most REMICs were structured as sequential classes, they quickly evolved to include many innovative classes. In fact, the cash flow structuring of multiclass securities had already become sophisticated and innovative during the prior three years of the CMO era. The REMIC legislation simply provided a legal framework for multiclass pass-throughs. The innovative classes includes PACs and support classes (supports), floaters and inverse floaters, IOs and POs, and VADMs (very accurately defined maturity bonds) and Z-bonds.

Planned Amortization Classes (PACs)

PACs were first introduced in late 1986. A PAC is structured to receive only a predetermined amount of principal cash flow under a wide range of prepayment scenarios. If prepayments of the underlying collateral rise up to a certain level, a PAC will receive only a fixed amount of principal. Conversely, if prepayments decline, a PAC has priority over other classes in receiving its predetermined principal cash flow. Because of this design, a PAC behaves almost like a corporate bond, with a great deal of certainty in average life and maturity.

Exhibit 2: Bloomberg Screen of Price/Yield Analysis and Cash Flow Characteristics of FHR 1748 Class C

G35 **Mtge**   Y T

Bloomberg
CMO

FGLMC 8 M

F H R   1 7 4 8   C
3133T57K3   CMO:**PAC-1(11)**
8.501(310)39 WAC(WAM)WALA SEP96

8% 9/15/24   ADV:<PAGE>
[100   250   9/96]   NO Notes
88 <Go>

SEP 1mo	149P	8.6	9/30/94:	25,400,000	next pay 10/15/96 (monthly)	30/360	Cashflows
'96 3mo	189	10.7	9/15/96:	25,400,000	rcd date 9/30/96 (14 Delay)	created	9/ 3/96
6mo	258	14.3	factor 1.000000000000		accrual 9/ 1/96- 9/30/96	1stProj	10/15/96
12mo	248	13.0				Collat:	785 Pools
Life	204	9.3					

9/16/96

Y I E L D - T O - M A T U R I T Y

| | | 75 | 100 | 145 | 250 | 300 | 400 | 500 |
| Vary PRICE | 1 32 | 75 PSA | 100 PSA | 145 PSA | 250 PSA | 300 PSA | 400 PSA | 500 PSA |

DEAL: CUR GEO DIST (08/96): CA 22.2% NY 7.3% IL 4.8% NJ 4.7% FL 4.6% OTHER 56.4%

| 100-27 | 7.995 | 7.992 | 7.992 | 7.992 | 7.991 | 7.969 | 7.942 |

AvgLife	14.63	14.07	14.07	14.07	14.05	11.00	8.71
Mod Dur	8.26	8.05	8.05	8.05	8.05	6.96	5.97
DATEWindow	7/08- 8/15/23	9/06- 8/15/23	9/06- 8/15/23	9/06- 8/15/23	9/06- 5/15/24	7/04- 5/15/24	10/02- 4/15/24
Tsy Sprd I	+103/AL	+104/AL	+104/AL	+104/AL	+104/AL	+104/AL	+108/AL

	SEP96 AUG JUL JUN MAY APR MAR FEB JAN DEC95 NOV OCT95	Treasury Curve - BGN 17:15
100 CALL N	149 210 210 299 293 386 302 221 242 187 211 246	3mo 6mo -1- -2- -3- -5- -10- -30-
	8.6 11.9 11.7 16.4 15.9 20.6 15.8 11.4 12.2 9.3 10.3 11.8	5.30 5.51 5.88 6.30 6.49 6.68 6.92 7.11

Format# 1-YT 1%Cleanup

Source: BLOOMBERG Financial Markets

For example, Exhibit 2 shows the cash flow characteristics of FHR 1748 C (Class C). Class C is a PAC backed by seasoned 30-year FHLMC Gold PC 8s. As of September 1996, at the current Bloomberg median speed of 145% PSA, Class C has an expected average life of 14.1 years. If the speed increases to 250% PSA or declines to 100% PSA, the expected average life of Class C remains unchanged at 14.1 years. The range of 100% to 250% PSA is called the *prepayment band* or the *PAC band*. Within this band, the average life of a Class C is protected against both shortening and lengthening. However, outside the band, Class C's average life still varies. At a 75% PSA, its average life lengthens slightly to 14.6 years; at 400% PSA, it shortens to 11 years.

It should be emphasized that the REMIC structure only reallocates the prepayment risk of the underlying collateral among various maturity classes; it cannot eliminate or even reduce the risk. The prepayment risk of PACs is reduced only because it is structurally shifted to other classes. The classes that absorb the prepayment risk of PACs are support classes. Exhibit 3 shows the cash flow of a support, FHR 1748 GE (Class GE). As of September 1996, at 145% PSA, the expected average life of Class GE is 18.6 years. However, at 100% PSA, the average life extends to 22.4 years. It extends further to 23.6 years at 75% PSA. Conversely, at 250% PSA, Class GE's average life shortens dramatically to just 1.9 years. It shortens further to 0.7 years at 400% PSA. The average lives of supports fluctuate violently because they are the prepayment "shock absorbers" of PACs.

Exhibit 3: Bloomberg Screen of Price/Yield Analysis and Cash Flow Characteristics of FHR 1748 Class GE

G35 **Mtge** Y T

Bloomberg CMO

FGLMC 8 M

F H R   1 7 4 8   G E
3133T5A78 CMO:**SUPPORT BOND**
8.501(310)39 WAC(WAM) WALA SEP96

8% 5/15/24 ADV:<PAGE>
NO Notes
88 <Go>

SEP 1mo	149P	8.6	9/30/94:	3,900,000	next pay 10/15/96 (monthly)	30/360 Cashflows
'96 3mo	189	10.7	9/15/96:	3,900,000	rcd date 9/30/96 (14 Delay)	created 9/ 3/96
6mo	258	14.3	factor 1.000000000000		accrual 9/ 1/96- 9/30/96	1stProj 10/15/96
12mo	248	13.0				Collat: 785 Pools
Life	204	9.3				

9/16/96

Y I E L D   T A B L E

		75	100	145	250	300	400	500
Vary PRICE	1 32	75 PSA	100 PSA	145 PSA	250 PSA	300 PSA	400 PSA	500 PSA

DEAL: CUR GEO DIST (08/96): CA 22.2% NY 7.3% IL 4.8% NJ 4.7% FL 4.6% OTHER 56.4%

98-15	8.255	8.257	8.266	8.849	9.267	10.083	10.927

AvgLife	23.58	22.36	18.64	1.93	1.18	0.67	0.47
Mod Dur	10.17	9.98	9.29	1.71	1.08	0.63	0.44
DATEWindow	12/19- 8/15/20	8/18- 7/15/19	8/14- 2/15/16	6/98-11/15/98	10/97- 1/15/98	4/97- 6/15/97	2/97- 3/15/97
Tsy Sprd I	+121/AL	+122/AL	+127/AL	+258/AL	+331/AL	+444/AL	+544/AL

	SEP96	AUG	JUL	JUN	MAY	APR	MAR	FEB	JAN	DEC95	NOV	OCT95	Treasury Curve - BGN 17:17
NEVER CALLED	149	210	210	299	293	386	302	221	242	187	211	246	3mo 6mo -1- -2- -3- -5- -10- -30-
	8.6	11.9	11.7	16.4	15.9	20.6	15.8	11.4	12.2	9.3	10.3	11.8	5.30 5.51 5.88 6.30 6.49 6.68 6.92 7.11

Format# 1-YT 1%Cleanup

Source: BLOOMBERG Financial Markets

PACs were warmly received by investors at the outset. In particular, insurance companies, which needed mortgage securities with more stable average lives than sequentials, purchased the bulk of PACs. In the late 1980s, PACs were refined to include Tier-I and Tier-II PACs (PAC Is and PAC IIs, the former having greater prepayment protection than the latter), TACs (targeted amortization classes with a certain degree of prepayment protection against shortening, but not against lengthening), and VADMs. (A class of "very accurately defined maturity" constitutes a very small portion of a REMIC because it uses the accrued interest from the Z-bond to accurately retire its principal on schedule.)

Floaters

Floaters also made their capital market debut in late 1986. Indexed initially to LIBOR, they were issued to meet the demand of commercial banks and foreign investors that had LIBOR-based liabilities. At the beginning, floaters were offered (with floating-rate residuals) without the pairing of inverse floaters. However, technology and marketing quickly developed to pair floaters with inverse floaters. The variety of indexes used for floaters also expanded to include COFI, various constant-maturity Treasuries (CMTs), yields on certificates of deposits (CDs), and the prime rate.

For example, Exhibit 4 shows that FNR 1993-224 FJ (Class FJ) is a LIBOR-indexed floater with a coupon reset formula: coupon rate = LIBOR + 50 basis points. As of July 1996, it has an original and current principal of $20,790,250 (the factor is 1.0000). Since the one-month LIBOR at the last coupon reset was 5.4688%, the current coupon rate of the floater is 5.4688% + 0.5% = 5.9688%. At a price of 98¹⁶⁄₃₂ and a speed of 110% PSA, Class FJ has an expected average life of 10.3 years and a "discount margin" of 69.7 basis points. Since at any given point in time the total interest payment of the collateral is fixed, the floater has to have a cap on the upward adjustment of its coupon. Class FJ has a cap (maximum coupon rate) of 10% and a floor (minimum rate coupon rate) of 0.5%.

Exhibit 4: Bloomberg Screen of Price/Yield Analysis and Cash Flow Characteristics of FNR 1993-224 Class FJ

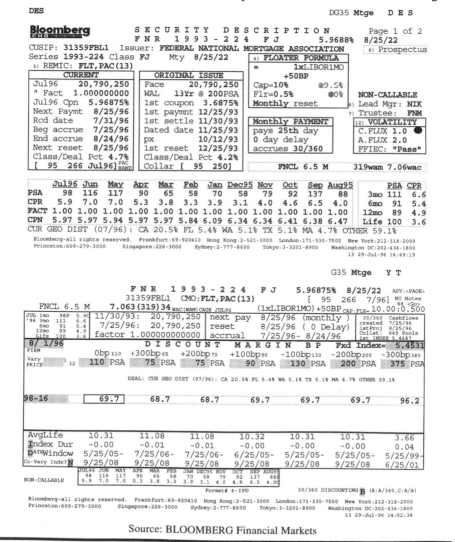

Source: BLOOMBERG Financial Markets

Exhibit 5: Bloomberg Screen of Price/Yield Analysis and Cash Flow Characteristics of FNR 1993-224 Class SJ

```
DES                                                      DG35 Mtge   D E S

Bloomberg              S E C U R I T Y   D E S C R I P T I O N      Page 1 of 2
CHO                    F N R   1 9 9 3 - 2 2 4   S J    7.4866%     8/25/22
CUSIP: 31359FBM9  Issuer: FEDERAL NATIONAL MORTGAGE ASSOCIATION    8) Prospectus
Series 1993-224 Class SJ   Mty 8/25/22    4) FLOATER FORMULA
5) REMIC: INV,PAC(13)                     =-1.85714xLIBOR1MO
     CURRENT              ORIGINAL ISSUE        +1764.285BP
Jul96    11,194,750   Face      11,194,750  Cap=17.6429%   @0%
" Fact 1.000000000    WAL     13Yr @ 200PSA  Flr=0%        @9.5%   NON-CALLABLE
Jul96 Cpn 7.48659%    1st coupon11.72321%   Monthly reset       6) Lead Mgr: NIK
Next Paymt 8/25/96    1st paymnt 12/25/93                        7) Trustee:  FNM
Rcd date  7/31/96     1st settle 11/30/93   Monthly PAYMENT      12) VOLATILITY
Beg accrue 7/25/96    Dated date 11/25/93   pays 25th day        C.FLUX 17.2
End accrue 8/24/96    px       10/12/93     0 day delay          A.FLUX 20.6
Next reset 8/25/96    1st reset 12/25/93    accrues 30/360       FFIEC: "Fail"
Class/Deal Pct 2.5%   Class/Deal Pct 2.2%
[  95  266 Jul96]PAC  Collar [  95  250]       FNCL 6.5 M      319wam 7.06wac
         BAND
```

	Jul96	Jun	May	Apr	Mar	Feb	Jan	Dec95	Nov	Oct	Sep	Aug95		PSA	CPR
PSA	98	116	117	90	65	58	70	58	79	92	137	88	3mo	111	6.6
CPR	5.9	7.0	7.0	5.3	3.8	3.3	3.9	3.1	4.0	4.6	6.5	4.0	6mo	91	5.4
FACT	1.00	1.00	1.00	1.00	1.00	1.00	1.00	1.00	1.00	1.00	1.00	1.00	12mo	89	4.9
CPN	7.49	7.49	7.54	7.49	7.49	7.72	7.25	6.79	6.79	6.67	6.73	6.56	Life	100	3.6

```
CUR GEO DIST (07/96): CA 20.5% FL 5.4% WA 4.7% OTHER 59.1%
```

```
YT79                                                     DG35 Mtge    Y T

             F N R   1 9 9 3 - 2 2 4   S J   7.48659%  8/25/22  ADV:<PAGE>
             31359FBM9  CMO:INV,PAC(13)         [ 95  266  7/96] NO Notes
FNCL 6.5 M    7.063(319)34 WAC(WAM)CAGE JUL96  (-1.85714xLIBOR1MO)+1764.285BP CAP:FLR=17.64:0.000
JUL 1mo  98P 5.9 11/30/93: 11,194,750  next pay 8/25/96 (monthly )  30/360 Cashflows
'96 3mo 111 6.6                                                     created 7/25/96
    6mo  91 5.4  7/25/96:  11,194,750  reset   8/25/96 ( 0 Delay)  1stProj 8/25/96
    12mo 89 4.9  factor 1.000000000    accrual 7/25/96- 8/24/96    Collat: 640 Pools
    Life 100 3.6                                                   1st INDEX 5.4688
8/ 1/96                        Y I E L D   T A B L E           Fxd Index= 5.4531
FIRM        0bp110  +300bp65  +200bp75  +100bp90  -100bp130  -200bp200  -300bp380
Vary    1 32  110 PSA   75 PSA   75 PSA   90 PSA   130 PSA   200 PSA   375 PSA
PRICE
        DEAL: CUR GEO DIST (07/96): CA 20.5% FL 5.4% WA 5.1% TX 5.1% MA 4.7% OTHER 59.1%

79   [11.180]  11.017   11.017   11.178   11.180   11.180   15.529

AvgLife      10.31      11.08     11.08    10.32    10.31     10.31     3.66
Sprd Dur      6.36       6.66      6.66     6.37     6.36      6.36     2.88
DATEWindow  5/25/05-   7/25/06-  7/25/06- 6/25/05- 5/25/05-  5/25/05-  5/25/99-
Co-Vary Indx? N 9/25/08  9/25/08  9/25/08  9/25/08  9/25/08   9/25/08   6/25/01
        JUL96 JUN MAY APR MAR FEB JAN DEC95 NOV OCT SEP AUG95   Treasury Curve - BGN 14:51
        98 116 117 90 65 58 70 58 79 92 137 88   3mo 6mo -1- -2- -3- -5- -10- -30-
        5.9 7.0 7.0 5.3 3.8 3.3 3.9 3.1 4.0 4.6 6.5 4.00  5.34 5.55 5.92 6.33 6.48 6.70 6.92 7.09
NON-CALLABLE            Format# 3-IPY        30/360 DISCOUNTING B (A:A/360,C:A/A)
```

Source: BLOOMBERG Financial Markets

Again, given the fixed coupon rate of the collateral, the fluctuation of coupon interest of a floater has to be offset by another maturity class that behaves as a companion to the floater: an inverse floater. Exhibit 5 shows FNR 1993-224 SJ (Class SJ), the inverse floater that is structurally "paired with" Class FJ. However, it has a smaller original and current principal of $11,194,750. Its coupon reset formula is: coupon rate = 1764.285 basis points $- 1.85714 \times$ LIBOR. Given the 5.4688% LIBOR at the last reset, the current coupon rate of Class SJ is: $0.1764285 - 1.85714 \times 0.054688 = 7.4866\%$. At a price of 79 and 110% PSA, Class SJ also has an expected average life of 10.3 years (which is exactly the same as that of Class FJ) with a yield of 11.18%.

The coefficient of the LIBOR index, 1.85714, is called "the multiplier (M)" of the inverse floater. At each reset, the change in LIBOR for the coupon of the floater is offset by a change of 1.85714 × LIBOR for the coupon of the inverse floater. Because of this multiplier, the inverse floater needs to have only a much smaller principal amount to offset the coupon fluctuation of the floater. In fact, the multiplier is precisely the ratio of principal amount of the floater to the inverse floater. The magnitude of the multiplier measures the leverage of the inverse floater. The larger the multiplier, the greater will be the leverage — and thus the fluctuation of the coupon of the inverse floater.[1]

Floaters were an instant success. LIBOR-indexed floaters quickly became a favorite investment of banks and foreign investors. Thrifts, on the other hand, overwhelmingly favored COFI-indexed floaters.[2] In the early years, floaters were basically structured as sequentials or PACs in terms of principal paydown. Recently, their structures have extended to include a significant amount of supports.

Interest-Only and Principal-Only Securities (IOs and POs)

The concept of stripping mortgage pass-throughs was developed in the early 1980s, although the actual issuance of IOs and POs first occurred in 1986. The idea of stripping pass-throughs came from the trading of servicing cash flows, which consisted of a strand of roughly 40 to 70 basis points of interest from the underlying mortgages. Because interest is generated from principal, the value of the servicing cash flow depends greatly on the size of the outstanding balance of mortgages. It is very sensitive to changes in market interest rates. In a rising interest rate environment, as prepayments are slow with a longer-lasting amount of outstanding balance, the servicing cash flow has a greater value. Conversely, in times of declining interest rates, as the outstanding balance of a mortgage pool depletes quickly by rapid prepayments, the servicing cash flow losses value.

Thus, unlike regular fixed-income securities, the value of servicing cash flows depreciated with declining interest rates but appreciated with rising interest rates. They were an ideal hedging vehicle against rising interest rates. To magnify their effectiveness as a hedge, servicing cash flows were modified and expanded to cover the entire coupon, or interest-only (IO), of pass-throughs.

Exhibit 6 illustrates the unique value of IOs, as represented by FNS 254 2. (For all FNMA stripped securities, FNS, "1" represents PO; "2," IO.) The IO is backed by 30-year FNMA 7.5s. At a price of 34 and a speed of 125% PSA, the IO has an expected average life of 9 years and yields 12.32%. But if interest rates rise 300 basis points, prepayment of FNMA 7.5s will decline significantly and the IO's yield will increase dramatically. At a 75% PSA, the yield rises to 15.67%.

[1] In recent years volatile interest rates coupled with the lack of liquidity and poor performance of inverse floaters have prompted investors to recombine floaters and inverse floaters into fixed-rate classes. The recombination is often accomplished through a process called "re-REMIC." Classes FJ and SJ can be recombined into a fixed rate class with a coupon of 6.5% and principal amount of $31,985,000 (the sum of principal of the two classes, $20,790,250 + $11,194,750). The fixed coupon rate is arrived by a recombination formula: $5.9688\% \times [1 / (1 + M)] + 7.4866\% \times [M / (1 + M)] = 6.5\%$.
[2] The significance of COFI for thrifts is discussed in Chapter 6.

Conversely, if interest rates decline and prepayments accelerate, IOs will lose value. At a 200% PSA, the yield of the IO drops quickly to 7.20%. It actually becomes −5.3% at a speed of 375% PSA.

By contrast, the PO behaves in just the opposite manner. At a price of 65 and a speed of 125% PSA, the PO yields 5.58% (Exhibit 7). If interest rates decline 100 basis points and prepayments increase to 200% PSA, its yield will rise to 7.99%. But if interest rates rise 100 basis points and prepayments drop slightly to 108% PSA, its yield will also decline to 5.09%.

Exhibit 6: Bloomberg Screen of Price/Yield Analysis and Cash Flow Characteristics of FNS 254 Class 2 (IO)

G35 **Mtge**   Y T

FNS 254 2 — 7.5% 1/1/24 — ADV:<PAGE>, Notes 88 <Go>

31364HG27   CMO: IO, NTL

FNCL 7.5 M — 7.915 (316) 37 WAC (WAM) CAGE JUL96

JUL 1mo 161P 9.70	1/28/94: 2359000000	next pay 8/25/96 (monthly)	30/360 Cashflows
'96 3mo 160 9.6	7/25/96: 1916858551	rcd date 7/31/96 (24 Delay)	created 7/12/96
6mo 151 8.9	factor 0.812572510000	accrual 7/1/96- 7/31/96	1stProj 8/25/96
12mo 142 7.9			Collat: 1513 Pools
Life 168 7.0			

7/23/96

YIELD TABLE

FIRM	0bp 130	+300bp 75	+200bp 90	+100bp 110	-100bp 200	-200bp 380	-300bp 475
Vary **32** 1 32 PRICE	**125 PSA**	**75 PSA**	**90 PSA**	**108 PSA**	**200 PSA**	**375 PSA**	**475 PSA**
31	14.623	18.000	16.992	15.777	9.452	-3.165	-10.77
32	13.809	17.175	16.171	14.959	8.654	-3.922	-11.50
33	13.043	16.399	15.398	14.190	7.904	-4.634	-12.19
34	**12.321**	**15.667**	**14.669**	**13.464**	**7.197**	**-5.305**	**-12.84**
35	11.638	14.975	13.980	12.779	6.528	-5.939	-13.45
36	10.992	14.320	13.327	12.130	5.895	-6.539	-14.03
37	10.379	13.699	12.709	11.514	5.295	-7.108	-14.58
AvgLife	9.01	11.50	10.66	9.76	6.56	3.72	2.90
Mod Dur	4.14	4.08	4.10	4.12	4.22	4.45	4.60
DATE Window	8/96- 1/25/24	8/96- 1/25/24	8/96- 1/25/24	8/96- 1/25/24	8/96- 1/25/24	8/96- 1/25/24	8/96- 1/25/24
Tsy Sprd I	+553/AL	+882/AL	+783/AL	+664/AL	+52/AL	-lge/AL	-lge/AL

JUL96	JUN	MAY	APR	MAR	FEB	JAN	DEC95	NOV	OCT	SEP	AUG95	Treasury Curve - BGN 11:00
161	168	152	165	142	117	111	133	139	156	143H	3mo 6mo -1- -2- -3- -5- -10- -30-
NON-CALLABLE	9.7	10.0	9.0	9.7	8.3	6.7	6.3	6.1	7.2	7.3	7.9 7.0C	5.27 5.49 5.77 6.22 6.40 6.61 6.83 7.03

Format# 1-YT

Source: BLOOMBERG Financial Markets

Exhibit 7: Bloomberg Screen of Price/Yield Analysis and Cash Flow Characteristics of FNS 254 Class 1 (PO)

G35 **Mtge**   Y T

FNS 254 1 — 0% 1/1/24 — ADV:<PAGE>, Notes 88 <Go>

31364HF93   CMO: PRINCIPAL ONLY CLASS

FNCL 7.5 M — 7.915 (316) 37 WAC (WAM) CAGE JUL96

JUL 1mo 161P 9.70	1/28/94: 2359000000	next pay 8/25/96 (monthly)	30/360 Cashflows
'96 3mo 160 9.6	7/25/96: 1916858551	rcd date 7/31/96 (24 Delay)	created 7/12/96
6mo 151 8.9	factor 0.812572510000	accrual 7/1/96- 7/31/96	1stProj 8/25/96
12mo 142 7.9			Collat: 1513 Pools
Life 168 7.0			

7/23/96

YIELD TABLE

FIRM	0bp 130	+300bp 75	+200bp 90	+100bp 110	-100bp 200	-200bp 380	-300bp 475
Vary **32** 1 32 PRICE	**125 PSA**	**75 PSA**	**90 PSA**	**108 PSA**	**200 PSA**	**375 PSA**	**475 PSA**
62	6.316	4.735	5.183	5.751	9.088	16.847	21.962
63	6.064	4.554	4.982	5.525	8.712	16.124	21.009
64	5.820	4.378	4.787	5.305	8.348	15.427	20.090
65	**5.582**	**4.206**	**4.596**	**5.091**	**7.995**	**14.752**	**19.202**
66	5.351	4.038	4.411	4.883	7.653	14.099	18.343
67	5.127	3.874	4.230	4.680	7.321	13.467	17.512
68	4.908	3.715	4.054	4.483	6.998	12.855	16.709
AvgLife	9.01	11.50	10.66	9.76	6.56	3.72	2.90
Mod Dur	6.57	9.06	8.19	7.29	4.43	2.32	1.76
DATE Window	8/96- 1/25/24	8/96- 1/25/24	8/96- 1/25/24	8/96- 1/25/24	8/96- 1/25/24	8/96- 1/25/24	8/96- 1/25/24
Tsy Sprd I	-119/AL	-263/AL	-223/AL	-172/AL	+133/AL	+829/AL	1283/AL

JUL96	JUN	MAY	APR	MAR	FEB	JAN	DEC95	NOV	OCT	SEP	AUG95	Treasury Curve - BGN 11:07
161	168	152	165	142	117	111	133	139	156	143H		3mo 6mo -1- -2- -3- -5- -10- -30-
NON-CALLABLE	9.7 10.0	9.0	9.7	8.3	6.7	6.3	6.1	7.2	7.3	7.9	7.00	5.29 5.49 5.79 6.21 6.39 6.59 6.82 7.00

Format# 1-YT

Source: BLOOMBERG Financial Markets

THE RISE AND FALL OF REMICS

The Rise of REMICs

The rapid growth of REMICs was attributable to constant innovations of REMIC classes to satisfy investor demands. While the creation of REMICs addresses the prepayment risk of mortgages by segmenting their cash flows into many maturity classes, it by no means reduces the overall risk of the collateral. It only reallocates the risk among various classes. The prepayment risk of one class is lowered only by raising the risk of another. The average-life certainty of a PAC is achieved by the creation of a corresponding support to absorb the prepayment fluctuation that would have been borne by the PAC. The more aggressively a PAC is structured to have average-life stability in a wide range of prepayment scenarios, the more volatile the average life of its companion support will be. Whenever a floater is created, the fluctuation of its coupon is offset by an inverse floater. Given the size of floating-rate principal within a deal, the larger the portion of a floater, the greater the coupon leverage of the inverse floater will be. Whenever the structuring of PACs and floaters becomes overly aggressive, the prepayment and interest rate risks of their companions are simply compounded. But, as voluminous REMICs with increasingly aggressive structures were churned out in the late 1980s and the early 1990s, the compounded risks were concealed by the steady declines in interest rates during that period. On the surface, the REMIC market enjoyed the spectacular growth that was the envy of other fixed-income securities.

The Fall of REMICs

By 1992-93, the creation of PACs and floaters turned too aggressive and too innovative for the good of the REMIC market. Their companions became so exotic that they were purchased only by a limited number of investors who eagerly pursued the hyped-up yields of these "exotic derivatives" despite the compounded risks. Worse, the structuring of some REMICs turned overly zealous: not only did they contain several dozen maturity classes, but many of them were exotic supports, inverse IOs (essentially interest-only portions of inverse floaters), and support inverse floaters. These classes attracted only a few investors. Their liquidity was restricted and they were doomed to fail. In April 1994, the sudden rise in interest rates and the dramatic escalation of volatility finally brought on the inevitable collapse of exotic REMICs. In just a few weeks, their prices nearly halved as their expected average lives extended substantially. Inverse floaters saw their coupon rates drop virtually to zero. Many investors who purchased these securities heavily in a highly leveraged fashion were driven to bankruptcy by margin calls. Dealers suffered huge losses on these securities and became reluctant to make markets for these securities. Liquidity of exotic REMICs evaporated and their prices fell still further. The failure of the exotic classes eventually brought down the whole REMIC market.

PROSPECTS FOR THE REMIC MARKET

Since its collapse in early 1994, the REMIC market has had more than two years to heal at the time of this writing. The market has learned its lesson, and issuance of REMICs showed signs of recovery in early 1996. There are two fundamental reasons to believe that the REMIC market will continue to recover. The recovery, however, will take the form of more simplified REMICs. The yield spread relationships among various classes will also be realigned.

First, the evolution of the market suggests that there are investors for mortgage securities with specifically structured cash flows. The technology of structuring multiclass mortgage securities has been well developed. Investors, who have grown accustomed to tailor-made mortgage securities, will have a continued demand for these securities. For example, the large number of floater investors has been well established. They will not disappear. Similarly, for regulatory and accounting reasons, banks and thrifts need to invest in assets such as short average-life PACs that roughly match their liabilities. For the same reason, insurance companies need to purchase intermediate or long average-life PACs. Pension funds have a special appetite for the longest average-life assets, such as Z-bonds. In order to satisfy their demands, PACs and Z-bonds will have to be issued. Also, to hedge against rising interest rates, there will be demand for IOs. As long as all these demands exist, the REMIC market has an investor base with which to recover.

Second, the enormous future demand for mortgage credit will require a proved efficient way of financing. For the balance of the 1990s, based on current demand for housing and housing price appreciation, mortgage originations to facilitate housing starts and existing home sales are projected to be around $500 billion annually. This amount plus originations for refinancing and other miscellaneous purposes (e.g., taking a second mortgage to pay for children's college education) will put annual originations in the neighborhood of $700 billion annually. History has proved that multiclass pass-throughs are the most efficient form of mortgage finance. Time will not roll back. REMICs will be issued to finance the enormous future demand for mortgage credit.

While the REMIC market is expected to recover, the pricing and the structuring of individual classes will change. Yield spreads of newly offered PACs will have to tighten. The substantial cheapening of supports suggests that investors have not been adequately compensated for all the risk associated with the securities. Supports are exceedingly risky, not only in terms of average-life variation but also in secondary-market liquidity. While large yield spreads of supports are primarily a reward for absorbing the prepayment fluctuation of PACs, in the future they will have to be compensated for the liquidity risk as well. To do so, greater yield spreads of supports will necessitate correspondingly tighter yield spreads for PACs.

Additionally, future PACs will be offered with more conservative prepayment bands. Structurally, aggressive PACs with wide bands and great prepayment protection can only be produced with their companion supports of substantial average-life fluctuation. These classes experienced the worst price depreciation during the recent derivative market debacle. To the extent that investors are no longer willing to assume the greater prepayment risk of supports, PACs with conservatively structured bands will be offered.

For the same reason, discount margins of floaters will have to tighten in order to enhance yields of inverse floaters. Also, for a given size REMIC, a floater of a smaller principal amount will be offered. Structurally, the size of a floater is proportional to the multiplier of its companion inverse floater. To offer a large floater, the multiplier of the inverse floater must increase correspondingly. Again, in the disarrayed secondary market, the price of high-multiplier inverse floaters suffered most severely. This experience suggests that few highly leveraged inverse floaters will be offered in the future.

CURRENT TRADING OF REMICS

One of the fundamental reasons for multiclass securities is to segment mortgage cash flows and price them along the Treasury yield curve. For that reason, REMIC classes trade in terms of yield spreads over the comparable average life Treasuries. The magnitude of the yield spread of a REMIC class reflects primarily the degree of its prepayment risk. As will be discussed in detail in Chapter 10, the yield spread measures the relative value of a bond class versus its comparable Treasury and other REMIC classes. Many factors influence the yield spread, including the specific cash flow structure of the bond class, the supply/demand situation, the level of interest rates, and the collateral yield spread. Here, yield spreads of various REMICs are presented to indicate their liquidity in trading.

Unlike single-class pass-throughs, REMICs are traded on yield spreads, not prices. For example, Exhibit 8 shows that as of September 12, 1996, a trader will bid or offer a 2-year PAC by quoting a yield spread of 34 basis points (bid) or 31 basis points (offer) over the 2-year Treasury yield at a certain speed. There are many 2-year PACs with different coupons, and they are also backed by various forms of collateral. It is impossible to quote a generic price. However, it is possible to quote a generic yield spread. Based on the generic yield spread, the price of a specific 2-year PAC can be derived from its yield, which is the sum of the yield spread and the 2-year Treasury yield. The bid-offer yield spreads of REMIC classes in Exhibit 8 are generic. They are representatives of newly issued PACs and sequentials backed by 30-year 6.5s and 7s.

The 3 basis point bid-offer yield spread differential of 2-year PACs measures their liquidity in trading. (REMICs are in general liquid, although not as liquid as single-class pass-throughs.) Bid-offer differentials of shorter average life PACs (short PACs) are tighter than their longer average life counterparts (long PACs), suggesting the long PACs are not as liquid as short PACs. One reason is that shorter PACs have a lower risk of collateral prepayments falling outside PAC bands than do long PACs. Also, short PACs have lower yields, hence proportionally tighter yield spreads. For these reasons, bid-offer differentials of PACs are slightly tighter than those of sequentials.

Exhibit 8: Bid-Offer Yield Spreads of Selected REMIC Classes, as of September 12, 1996

Average Life (year)	PACs (basis point)	Sequentials (basis point)
2	34 - 31	72 - 67
3	35 - 32	79 - 74
5	46 - 42	83 - 78
7	68 - 62	100 - 94
10	69 - 63	110 - 103
20	72 - 68	120 - 113

Note: Yield spreads are indicative of REMICs backed by generic new production 30-year 6.5s and 7s whose yield spreads average 95 basis points over the 10-year Treasury.

Source: Oppenheimer & Co., Inc.

Yield spreads of supports are wider than those of sequentials. Because they are structured to absorb the prepayment fluctuation of PACs, their average lives are very sensitive to the pricing speeds of PACs. The assumption of collateral prepayments is critically important in trading of supports. Since there are usually wide differences in prepayment assumptions, the yield spread quotes of supports vary significantly (and therefore they are not included in Exhibit 8). The bid-offer yield spread differentials are also greater than those of PACs and sequentials. In general, the more exotic the cash flow structure of REMICs, the wider the bid-offer yield spread differential will be.

PSA PREPAYMENT CURVE REVISITED

As mentioned in Chapter 4, the PSA prepayment curve implicitly assumes that new pass-throughs are backed exclusively by "housing-mortgages" — those that are originated to facilitate housing transactions. Because of this assumption, the PSA prepayment curve has a 30-month "ramp period." This period basically recognizes that newly moved-in mortgagors are likely to remain at the residence for the first few years. Therefore, from a housing transaction point of view, the PSA curve allows only a gradual increase in prepayments as the underlying mortgagors begin moving again. The assumption became questionable as a result of rampant refinancing in 1993. Voluminous higher-coupon pass-throughs were refinanced in 1993 by newly issued ones that carry a 6.5% to 7.5% coupon rate. It was estimated that nearly 60% of the $510 billion newly issued agency-guaranteed fixed-rate pass-throughs were backed by "refinancing mortgages" — those that are originated to facilitate refinancing.

The "refinancing mortgagors" by definition are homeowners who were already occupants of the houses on which the mortgages were originated. They may well be "seasoned" homeowners and, in that case, much more likely to prepay their "new" mortgages early on by selling their houses than housing-originated mortgagors. Judging by the level of mortgage rates that prevailed in the early 1990s, refinancing mortgagors are likely to have been homeowners for at least one year when they refinanced. By contrast, "housing-mortgagors" are brand new occupants of the houses on which mortgages are originated. They are unlikely to move within the first few years of occupancy.

As a result of rampant refinancing, there is a need to modify the ramp of the PSA curve as a yardstick for measuring prepayment speeds of new pass-throughs. By taking into consideration that new pass-throughs are backed by a significant amount of refinancing-mortgages, the ramp of the PSA curve should be modified to have a much flatter slope. The ramp period, however, remains unchanged to recognize that new mortgage pools are also represented by a significant number of "housing mortgagors."

A Modified Ramp

Assuming homeowners who refinanced their mortgages had already occupied their houses for at least 30 months, the ramp of the PSA curve can be easily modified to measure prepayments of newly issued pass-throughs in 1993. Based on the estimated volume of refinance- and housing-mortgages in 1993 (60% versus 40%), Exhibits 9 and 10 show a new 100% PSA curve with a modified ramp to account for the overwhelming presence of refinancing-mortgages in the pool of a newly issued fixed-rate pass-through.

Exhibit 9: Structuring a Modified PSA Ramp of a Newly Issued Fixed-Rate Pass-Throughs Backed by 60% Refinancing and 40% Housing Mortgages

Age (months)	New Mortgage CPR (%)	Refinancing Mortgage CPR (%)	Modified Ramp CPR (%)	Age (months)	New Mortgage CPR (%)	Refinancing Mortgage CPR (%)	Modified Ramp CPR (%)
1	0.2	6.0	3.68	16	3.2	6.0	4.88
2	0.4	6.0	3.76	17	3.4	6.0	4.96
3	0.6	6.0	3.84	18	3.6	6.0	5.04
4	0.8	6.0	3.92	19	3.8	6.0	5.12
5	1.0	6.0	4.00	20	4.0	6.0	5.20
6	1.2	6.0	4.08	21	4.2	6.0	5.28
7	1.4	6.0	4.16	22	4.4	6.0	5.36
8	1.6	6.0	4.24	23	4.6	6.0	5.44
9	1.8	6.0	4.32	24	4.8	6.0	5.52
10	2.0	6.0	4.40	25	5.0	6.0	5.60
11	2.2	6.0	4.48	26	5.2	6.0	5.68
12	2.4	6.0	4.56	27	5.4	6.0	5.76
13	2.6	6.0	4.64	28	5.6	6.0	5.84
14	2.8	6.0	4.72	29	5.8	6.0	5.92
15	3.0	6.0	4.80	30	6.0	6.0	6.00

Source: Oppenheimer & Co., Inc.

Exhibit 10: A Modified versus a Current 100% PSA Curve

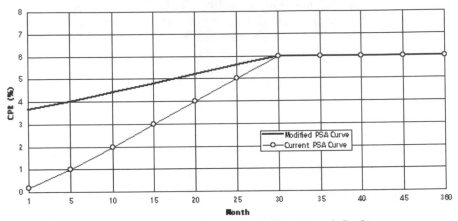

Sources: Public Securities Association and Oppenheimer & Co., Inc.

Because 60% of the underlying mortgages are refinancing related, their prepayment rate is expected to be always 6% CPR at a 100% PSA. The weighted prepayment rate for the first month of the pass-through is therefore 3.68% CPR. (That is the sum of 60% of 6% CPR and 40% of 0.2% CPR.) As the pass-through ages, its prepayment rate will rise gradually following the current PSA pattern to allow for the aging of the 40% of the pass-through that is still backed by housing-mortgagors. But the monthly increase in the prepayment rate will be much more moderate — only 40% of the 0.2% CPR, or 0.08% CPR. By the 30th month, however, the prepayment rate still reaches 6% CPR.

To test whether the modified ramp resembles reality, we compare the current PSA ramp with the prepayment patterns of eight randomly selected REMICs that are backed by newly issued 30-year FNMA and FHLMC 7s. The original face of collateral of these deals totals $7.5 billion. As shown in Exhibit 11, newly issued pass-throughs have been prepaying much faster during the ramp period than suggested by the current PSA curve. The difference is particularly noticeable when the WAM shortens to below 355 months. This suggests that refinancing-mortgagors may have already occupied their houses for over 20 months. Between 344 and 354 months of WAM, the prepayment rates of the new collateral were generally two to four times faster than the current PSA ramp.

Underestimation of Cash Flow Yields of Discount Coupons

Based on the modified ramp, the bond-equivalent cash flow yield of discount coupons is markedly higher than that calculated on the current PSA ramp. This outcome is expected because for given prices of discount coupons, faster prepayments always raise yields. For example, as shown in Exhibit 12, a new 30-year FNMA 7% pass-through with a WAM of 360 months at a price of 92 on a

"160% modified PSA" yields 8.58% on a bond-equivalent basis. This "modified yield" is 10 basis points higher than the bond-equivalent cash flow yield calculated on a "160% current PSA." As the new pass-through ages (WAM shortens), this yield differential decreases because the gap between the modified and the current PSA ramps becomes increasingly smaller. When the WAM shortens to 330 months, the gap reduces to zero and the yield differential no longer exists.

Average-Life Overestimation and Underpricing of Short REMICs

The modified ramp has important implications on new pass-through backed REMICs, especially those with short average lives. Short REMICs are structured with the collateral's early principal cash flow. Since the current PSA curve underestimates this cash flow early on, their expected average lives are overestimated. For example, a three-year average life PAC based on the current PSA curve may have only an expected average life of two years with a much shorter window based on the modified PSA curve.

Exhibit 11: Prepayments of Collateral of Randomly Selected REMICs versus the PSA Ramp

WAM (month)	PSA Ramp CPR (%)	Prepayments in CPR (%)							
		FNR 93-70	FNR 93-112	FNR 93-116	FNR 93-195	FHR 1541	FHR 1593	FHR 1603	FHR 1663
359	0.2								
358	0.4								
357	0.6	0.7	0.6	0.8					
356	0.8	1.8	1.9		6.4	0.8		5.2	
355	1.0			1.6	10.4	3.3		12.9	
354	1.2	2.2	3.3	2.9		5.7	6.3		
353	1.4	4.2	5.5	4.0	6.1		13.5	8.8	4.4
352	1.6	9.2	7.9		4.1	10.2	11.7	5.9	
351	1.8	12.0		9.7	4.4	13.4		6.8	5.3
350	2.0		6.1	7.4		9.8	7.5		5.3
349	2.2	14.4	3.6	3.3	5.6		10.3	5.7	5.1
348	2.4	10.9	4.9	2.6		6.7		5.0	
347	2.6	4.9	4.6			7.3	7.1		
346	2.8			4.1		6.1	5.6		
345	3.0	5.6				5.7			
344	3.2	7.1							

Note: The first four REMICs are backed by 30-year FNMA 7s; the next four, 30-year FHLMC Gold 7s.
Source: BLOOMBERG Financial Markets.

Exhibit 12: Bond Equivalent Cash Flow Yield Differential Based on Current and Modified PSA Ramps of 30-Year FNMA 7s with a WAM of 360 months

Price	Current PSA Yield (%)	Modified PSA Yield (%)	Modified minus Current (bp)	Price	Current PSA Yield (%)	Modified PSA Yield (%)	Modified minus Current (bp)
90	8.89	9.02	13	100	7.02	7.01	−1
91	8.68	8.80	12	101	6.85	6.84	−1
92	8.48	8.58	10	102	6.69	6.66	−3
93	8.29	8.37	8	103	6.52	6.49	−3
94	8.10	8.17	7	104	6.36	6.32	−4
95	7.91	7.97	6	105	6.21	6.15	−6
96	7.73	7.77	4	106	6.05	5.99	−6
97	7.54	7.57	3	107	5.90	5.82	−8
98	7.37	7.38	1	108	5.75	5.67	−8
99	7.19	7.20	1	109	5.60	5.51	−9

Source: Oppenheimer & Co., Inc.

The average-life overestimation has the impact of underpricing securities. The underpricing could be substantial if the slope of the Treasury yield curve is steep. In 1993, the three-year Treasury on average yielded 40 basis points more than the two-year Treasury. For a two-year average life PAC to provide a three-year average life yield, its price has to be lowered by roughly ¾ of a point.

Exaggerating Speeds of New Pass-Throughs Issued in 1992 and 1993

Given that a realistic ramp of the PSA curve is much flatter than the current one, prepayments in 1993 were exaggerated in terms of PSA speeds for newly issued pass-throughs. These were mostly 6.5% to 8% pass-throughs backed by mortgages originated between 1991 and 1993 carrying a mortgage rate of 7% to 8.5%. More than 50% of the underlying mortgages backing these new pass-throughs were refinancing-mortgages.

To measure the overestimation of prepayment speeds, consider for example 1992 production of 30-year FNMA 7s. In November 1993, this pass-through had a WAM of 353 months and a prepayment rate of 9.5% CPR. Measured by the current PSA ramp, its speed was 679% PSA (9.5/1.4 × 100). But in terms of the modified ramp for new pass-throughs issued in 1993, this speed would have been 228% "modified PSA" (9.5/4.16 × 100), a whopping 451% PSA slower than the speed measured by the current PSA curve.

Chapter 8

Private-Label Mortgage-Backed Securities

- A Typical Transaction
- Characteristics of the Underlying Mortgages
- The Cash Flow Structure — Mechanism of Credit Enhancement
- Credit Rating Criteria
- Loss Experience
- The Importance of House Price Appreciation
- Prepayment Pattern
- Pricing and Trading

A TYPICAL TRANSACTION

In recent years, private-label pass-throughs (hereafter, private-label securities) have attracted considerable attention from investors. The credit of private-label securities is not guaranteed by any of the three federal agencies — Ginnie Mae, Fannie Mae, and Freddie Mac. While private-label securities have always been small in total issuance relative to those guaranteed by agencies (agency-guaranteed securities), they have gained significance in the REMIC market (see Exhibit 1). First issued in 1987, REMICs are mutliclass pass-throughs backed mostly by fixed-rate mortgages. While virtually all fixed-rate private-label securities were issued as REMICs, less than 80% of newly issued fixed-rate agency-guaranteed securities were in a multiclass format. Worse, following their collapse in 1994, agency REMICs accounted for only 8% of fixed-rate agency-guaranteed securities issued in 1995. Most significant, in 1995, issuance of private-label REMICs exceeded for the first time those guaranteed by agencies. Although agency REMICs have staged an impressive recovery in 1996, they still represent just 16% of newly issued fixed-rate agency-guaranteed securities.

As mentioned in Chapter 7, one important milestone in the securitization of residential mortgages was the creation of collateralized mortgage obligations (CMOs) that "maturity tranched" the underlying collateral cash flow. The REMIC provisions of the Tax Reform Act of 1986 enhanced the efficiency of securitization by allowing the issuer of mortgage securities to sell the underlying collateral as pass-throughs in a multiclass format. The mechanism of maturity tranching allows the issuer to price the collateral cash flow "along the Treasury yield curve." This pricing mechanism is far superior to that of single-class mortgage pass-throughs, whose entire cash flow was priced off just one spot on the long end of the curve. Since 1987, the key feature of agency-guaranteed securities has been the creative segmentation of the mortgage cash flow into various types of maturity classes to satisfy the varying demands of investors.

Private-label securities not only take advantage of the REMIC legislation for "maturity tranching," but also resort to "credit tranching" to improve the pricing of a majority portion of the collateral cash flow. Credit tranching is essentially dividing the collateral cash flow into various classes so that they individually can obtain the highest possible credit ratings. To describe a private-label security, this section presents a randomly selected but typical transaction, Norwest Asset Securities Corporation Mortgage Pass-Through Certificates, Series 1996-6 (Bloomberg ticker symbol: NSCOR 1996-6). This transaction is presented in two parts: the characteristics of underlying mortgages (Exhibit 2) and the cash flow structure of the security (Exhibit 3). All terminology will be explained after this section throughout this chapter.

As shown in Exhibit 2, mortgages backing NSCOR 1996-6 can be generally characterized as 30-year fixed-rate, single-family, owner-occupied mortgages with a weighted average maturity (WAM) of 359 months and a weighted average mortgage coupon rate (WAC) of 8.11%. These mortgages are secured primarily by houses located in four states: California (18% of all mortgages), New Jersey (16%), Georgia (7%), and Connecticut (7%). Additionally, the underlying mortgages were originated to accommodate relocating employees of major corporations. These loans have an exceedingly large original balance with a weighted average of $298,500. However, they have a rather normal weighted loan-to-value (LTV) ratio of just under 80%. A little over 22% of loans with LTVs exceeding 80% do not carry a mortgage insurance.

Exhibit 1: Annual Issuance of Agency-Guaranteed and Private-Label REMICs, 1988 to 1996*

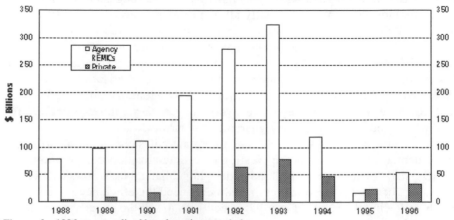

* Figures for 1996 are annualized based on nine-month data.
Source: Reprinted with permission of Inside Mortgage Securities, Copyright 1996, Bethesda, Maryland.
(301-951-1240)

Exhibit 2: Underlying Mortgage Characteristics of Norwest Asset Securities Corporation Mortgage Pass-Through Certificates, Series 1996-6

Purpose of Loans		Occupancy	
Purchase money		Owner-occupied	100%
Equity takeout		Renter-occupied	
Refinancing		Vacation	
Relocation	100%		
Type of Secured Property		**Geographic Dispersion**	
Single family	97.8%	California	18%
2-4 family		New Jersey	16%
Condominium	1.7%	Georgia	7%
PUD	0.4%	Connecticut	7%
Loan Term		**Loan Type**	
30-year	99.9%	Fixed-rate, level payment	100%
20-year	0.1%	Adjustable-rate	
WAM and WAC		Balloon	
WAM: 359 months	238 to 369 months	**Origination Year**	
Gross WAC: 8.11%	7.13% to 9.50%	1996	100%
Net WAC: 7.84%		1995	
Loan-to-Value Ratio		**Loan Size**	
Less than 80%	62.2%	Less than $210,000	0.6%
More than 80%	37.8%	$210,000 to $300,000	50.2%
Uninsured	22.8%	$300,000 to $480,000	39.7%
Weighted average:	78.7%	More than $480,000	9.7%
		Weighted average:	$298,500

Sources: Duff & Phelps Credit Rating Co. and BLOOMBERG Financial Markets

These loans were securitized by Norwest Asset Securities Corporation, the issuer of the security. For accounting and taxation purposes, the issuer elected REMIC status for the security. As shown in Exhibit 3, the first four maturity tranches of the security, A-1, A-2, A-PO, and A-R, have expected average lives of 5.63, 10.65, 5.82, and 0.08 years based on a pricing assumption of "100% PPC." The PPC, *prospectus prepayment curve*, is a transaction specific curve that assumes a flat speed of 150% PSA from months 1 through 12, and a flat speed of 300% PSA from months 13 through 360. This particular prepayment curve is used in this transaction because the underlying mortgages are relocation loans. (Some home equity loan backed transactions also use PPCs.) A detailed description of relocation loans will be provided in a later section. By maturity tranching, all "A" tranches are priced efficiently off the 5- and 10-year sectors of the Treasury yield curve. This way of pricing allows the underlying collateral to reach a greater price than simply off the 10-year spot of the Treasury curve.

Exhibit 3: Participating Entities and Cash Flow Structure of Norwest Asset Securities Corporation Mortgage Pass-Through Certificates, Series 1996-6

Originators: Norwest Mortgage, Inc. and Prudential Home Mortgage Company, Inc.
Issuer (Seller): Norwest Asset Securities Corporation
Servicers: Norwest Mortgage, Inc. (99.41% of loans) and Citicorp Mortgage (0.59%)
Master Servicer: Norwest Bank Minnesota, N.A.
Trustee: First Union National Bank of North Carolina

Tranche	Coupon (%)	Balance ($000s)	Wghted Average Life (yr.)	Description	Credit Rating	Type of Offering	Credit Support
A-1	7.5	94,048.3	5.63	Sr., Seq.	AAA	Public	4.50%
A-2	7.5	1,253.6	10.65	Non-ac. Sr.	AAA	Public	4.50%
A-PO	0	472.5	5.82	Sr., PO	AAA	Public	4.50%
A-R	7.5	0.1	0.08	Sr. Res.	AAA	Public	4.50%
M	7.5	1,755.0	10.65	Mez.	AA	Public	2.75%
B-1	7.5	1,504.0	10.65	Sub.	A	Public	1.25%
B-2	7.5	502.0	10.65	Sub.	BBB	Public	0.75%
B-3	7.5	250.0	N. A.	Sub.	BB	Private	0.50%
B-4	7.5	201.0	N. A.	Sub.	B	Private	0.30%
B-5	7.5	301.3	N. A.	Sub.	N. R.	Private	
Total		100,289					

Notes:
On May 1996, Norwest Mortgage, Inc. acquired all of the mortgage origination, servicing, and secondary marketing operations of the Prudential Home Mortgage Company, Inc.
The trustee also acts as the initial paying agent, certificate registrar, and custodian.
Sr. denotes senior; Seq., sequential tranche; PO, principal-only; Mez., mezzanine; Sub., subordinated; and Res., residual. Class A-2 is a non-accelerated sequential tranche.
The A and M classes also obtained similar ratings from Standard & Poor's Rating Group.
Sources: Duff & Phelps Credit Rating Co. and BLOOMBERG Financial Markets.

Equally important, the transaction utilizes a senior/subordinated cash flow structure for credit enhancement. The transaction's total of $100.3 million original principal balance is "credit tranched" with different credit ratings. All "A" tranches with original principal of $95.8 million, or 95.5% of the total transaction, are designed as the senior class. The credit of the senior class is enhanced by the cash flow of the remaining 4.5% of the collateral cash flow, which is further credit tranched into one mezzanine tranche and five subordinated tranches. These tranches are credit enhanced by an increasingly smaller amount of credit support.

Based on the characteristics of underlying mortgages and the structured credit support, all "A" and mezzanine tranches have obtained a triple-A and a double-A ratings, respectively from both Duff & Phelps Credit Rating Co. (DCR) and Standard & Poor's Ratings Group (Standard & Poor's). The B-1 to B-4 tranches also obtained a single-A to single-B ratings from DCR. The last tranche, B-5, is a "first loss" piece. It is structured to absorb all initial losses, up to 0.3%, of the original principal balance of the mortgage pool. The investment-grade tranches (triple-A to Triple-B) are offered publicly, the other tranches are placed privately.

CHARACTERISTICS OF THE UNDERLYING MORTGAGES

The fundamental difference between private-label and agency-guaranteed securities emanates from their underlying mortgages. As pointed out in Chapter 3, mortgages that are eligible for Ginnie Mae pools have to be newly originated (less than one-year old), either insured by FHA or guaranteed by VA. For Fannie Mae- or Freddie Mac-guaranteed securities, mortgages have to conform to the specifics of their mortgage underwriting and securitization programs (FHA and VA mortgages are also eligible.) Most important, the size of the mortgage in original loan balance cannot exceed the "conforming limit" posted annually by the two agencies. For single family mortgages, the 1996 limit is $207,000. Mortgage loans with an original balance exceeding this limit are termed "non-conforming" loans, or colloquially "jumbos." A substantial portion of loans underlying NSCOR 1996-6 far exceeded this limit. They range mostly between $210,000 and $480,000, averaging $298,500 on a principal weighted basis.

In addition to the original loan size, the following are three significant "non-conforming" factors that exclude mortgages from "agency pools."

High LTV
Agencies require that the ratio of original mortgage loan balance to the market value of the property be no higher than 80%. In other words, the mortgagor has to have at least a 20% down payment to purchase the house. If a mortgage's LTV exceeds 80%, it has to be insured by a primary mortgage insurance company such that the sum of the down payment and the mortgage insurance brings the LTV down to 75%. Uninsured mortgages with LTVs in excess of 80% can still be eligible for agency pools on a "negotiated basis." It entails arrangements such as recourse and self-insurance (by originators). Otherwise, uninsured loans with high LTVs are excluded from agency pools. Exhibit 2 shows that the LTV of 37.8% of the mortgages pooled for NSCOR 1996-6 exceeded 80%, and 22.8% of all mortgages had high LTVs with no mortgage insurance.

Lack of Full Documentation
The origination of a mortgage involves an extensive credit check of the mortgage applicant. Mortgage underwriting guidelines specified by agencies require documentation verifying the appraised value of the secured property, the applicant's credit history, sources of income, and history of employment. While agencies recognize that the method of verification may vary from one originator to another, they require that it be conducted in a consistent and professional manner. Mortgage loans originated without a complete verification of these aspects are often

referred to as "low doc" or "no doc" loans. Unless agreed on a negotiated basis, "low docs" and "no docs" are non-conforming loans.

Low Credit Quality of Borrower

A mortgage loan that has a low LTV and full documentation may still be non-conforming because the credit quality of the borrower does not meet the agencies' standards. Although there are no specific definitions of the quality standards, they are measured, as a general business practice, in terms of borrowers' credit history and *debt-to-income ratio* (a ratio of monthly mortgage payment to monthly after-tax income). For example, credit-rating agencies tend to define a borrower who has no prior bankruptcies and no delinquencies for credit card or any installment payments with a 36% debt-to-income ratio as an "A" quality borrower. Those who have prior bankruptcies and frequent delinquencies with a higher debt-to-income ratio are classified as "B," "C," or "D" borrowers. Agencies tend to exclude mortgages originated for below "A" quality borrowers from their pools.

Increasingly, in recent years, both originators and rating agencies have relied on models of "credit scores" to evaluate the credit quality of borrowers. In fact, the thinking among credit agencies has evolved to view the quality of the borrower as just as important as the LTV. Among the most popular scores, developed by Fair, Isaac, and Co., Inc. are the FICO scores. The scores are the collective output of three models: BEACON, TRW/FICO, and EMPIRICA. Various historical and current aspects of a borrower's credit, income, assets, liabilities, and employment are quantified into a score. Statistically, the score, as an index, has proven to be highly predictive of a borrower's risk of delinquency and default. The higher the score, the better is the quality of the borrower. For example, on a range of 400 (highest risk) to 900 (lowest risk), a FICO score of 660 or higher would place a borrower under the "A" category. A mortgage loan with a score lower than 620 is likely to be viewed by the agencies as non-conforming.

In addition to credit scores, rating agencies have also looked into mortgage scores of borrowers. A mortgage score includes not only variables of credit scores but also those specific to a mortgage, such as LTV, tenure of occupancy, purpose of mortgage, economic conditions of the location of property, employment of borrower, etc.

THE CASH FLOW STRUCTURE — MECHANISM OF CREDIT ENHANCEMENT

Non-conforming loans are not necessarily of lesser quality than conforming loans. In fact, as will be explained in more detail, research by Morgan Stanley has indicated that non-conforming loans have a slightly lower total delinquency rate than that of conventional mortgages. However, without an agency guarantee, the credit of a security backed by non-conforming loans without some arrangement of credit enhancement cannot obtain a top credit rating by the leading rating agencies. Over the past decade, the credit enhancement of private-label securities has evolved to include the following methods.

Senior/Subordinated Cash Flow Structure

The most popular means of credit enhancement is through "self insurance." That is, the security issuer segments the total principal cash flow generated from the mortgage pool into two classes: senior and subordinated. They are conventionally termed as A and B classes. Over the past seven years, between 48% and 92% of private-label securities resorted to the A/B structure for credit enhancement (Exhibit 4). As shown in Exhibit 2, NSCOR 1996-6 resorts to this structure by subordinating 4.5% of the total principal cash flow to enhance the credit of the senior class to a triple-A rating. This is a 95.5-4.5 A/B split. Under this arrangement, all the principal cash flow except scheduled amortization on a pro rata basis of 95.5-to-4.5 is to satisfy the senior class first before the subordinated class is paid. Class B is to absorb all losses until its balance is depleted to zero.

Increasingly, the A/B structure has included a mezzanine class (M) between the senior and the subordinated classes. NSCOR 1996-6 is an example of the A/M/B structure. While its cash flow is also subordinated to the A classes, the M class itself has a credit support of 2.75% of the total principal cash flow. For that support, the M class achieves a double-A credit rating. This structure takes advantage of the low credit risk of the underlying mortgages. As will be explained later, NSCOR 1996-6 is backed exclusively by relocation mortgages, which have proven to be of low credit risk. In fact, this very aspect enables even two B tranches, B-1 and B-2, to obtain investment-grade credit rating of single-A and triple-B, respectively.

Exhibit 4: Credit Enhancement of Private-Label Securities by Type, 1990-1996*

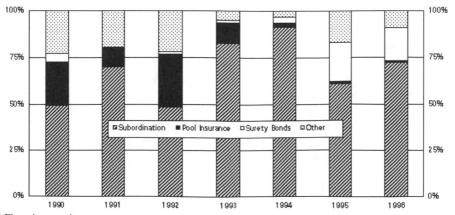

* First nine months

Source: Reprinted with permission of Inside Mortgage Securities, Copyright 1996, Bethesda, Maryland.
(301-951-1240)

Given that a portion of the underlying mortgages inevitably prepays through time, there is a built-in mechanism of *shifting interest* to gradually strengthen the credit support of the subordinated class. For example, for the first five years (a lockout period), this mechanism allocates all prepayments (but not amortized repayments) to retire the senior class. A 5-year lockout period is selected because historical data show that about 50% to 60% of all defaults of fixed-rate mortgages generally occur within the first five years after their originations. (Adjustable-rate mortgages have proven to be more risky than fixed-rate mortgages. The lockout period for ARM-backed mortgage securities, therefore, is usually 10 years.) As the principal balance of the senior class diminishes more quickly through prepayments and that of the subordinate class declines only marginally through amortization, the ratio of credit support rises during the lock-out period. NSCOR 1996-6 has a 5-year lockout period. During the lockout period, the A class will receive prepaid principal. The M and B classes will receive only amortized principal on a pro rata basis.

After the lockout, there will be a "step-down" period of another five years, where the M and the B classes will begin to receive a pro rata share of prepaid principal — a stepping down of their credit support to the A class. In each year of the step-down period, the shifting interest for the A class declines from 100% to 70%, 60%, 40%, 20%, and zero.

Bond Insurance

There are several monoline insurance companies whose only business is to insure bonds against possible losses. For mortgage securities, losses could be resulting from insufficient cash flow generated from the underlying mortgages to pay the interest and eventually to retire the bonds. (These bonds are called *surety bonds*.) When that happens, bond insurance companies provide up to as much as a 100% loss coverage. (For established issuers with good performance records in terms of delinquencies and defaults of their existing pools, the coverage ratio could be substantially less than 100%.)

However, bond insurers usually require private-label securities to have a combination of a *reserve account*, a certain degree of overcollateralization, and subordinated seller interest to take the first loss position. Bond insurers, such as MBIA, FGIC, CapMAC, and FSA, each have triple-A credit ratings from at least one of the top credit agencies, and their credit quality flows through to the securities they insure. Credit enhancement through bond insurance became popular in 1995 and 1996, when more than 18% of annual issues of private-label securities resorted to surety bonds (Exhibit 4). This share was substantially higher than that of 1990-94, when it was no greater than 5%.

Pool Insurance and Corporate Guarantee

The credit of a mortgage security can be enhanced by the guarantee of the corporate parent of its issuer or a mortgage insurance company in the form of pool insurance. Like bond insurance, the credit of the corporate parent or the mortgage insurance company flows through to the security. For that reason, this type of credit enhancement usually works when the guarantor or the insurer has a triple-A credit rating. Corporate guarantee was never a popular means of credit enhancement, although pool insurance was utilized by 11% to 28% of private-label securities issued in 1990-93. In recent years, however, this share has shrunk to less than 2%.

Letter of Credit

A fourth and a rare alternative of credit enhancement is a letter of credit (LOC) from a commercial bank with a triple-A credit rating. Like bond insurance, LOCs usually provide loss coverage after the reserve account. Also, the credit of LOC-insured securities is reflected by the credit quality of the LOC provider.

CREDIT RATING CRITERIA

As mentioned earlier, private-label securities have been increasingly issued with many "credit tranches." These tranches have been rated from triple-A to single-B with different rating criteria. NSCOR 1996-6 is a good example of "credit tranching." While the rating criteria for each credit category may differ in specific details among the four rating agencies (Standard & Poor's; DCR; Moody's Investors Service, "Moody's," and Fitch Investors Service, "Fitch"), they share a general theme. All rating agencies evaluate the potential risk of each credit tranche in terms of required loss coverage under worst-case scenarios, the characteristics of the underlying mortgage pool, and other considerations such as the quality of the issuer/servicer and the master servicer.

Required Loss Coverage

An overwhelming portion of the cash flow of private-label securities have obtained a triple-A credit rating from at least one rating agency. A triple-A rated class has to be able to withstand a severe economic recession. In such a worst-case scenario, housing prices plunge, unemployment soars and, as a result, mortgage delinquency and default become prevalent. A triple-A rated class needs an adequate loss coverage to prevent any losses of principal. To assess the severity of losses due to defaults, rating agencies make realistic assumptions about the foreclosure rate and loss severity.

The *foreclosure rate* is simply the annual percentage of a mortgage pool that will eventually default and go into foreclosure. The *loss severity* measures the realized loss as a percent of the mortgage pool's original loan balance at the completion of the foreclosure proceeding. The calculation of the loss severity entails two additional assumptions: the decline in market value of secured property at liquidation and the *foreclosure costs*. The foreclosure costs include brokerage fees for liquidating the secured property, maintenance of the property, all incurred legal costs, and accrued mortgage interest. Under all these assumptions, triple-A rated classes are still protected under the specific arrangement of credit enhancement. For example, for a triple-A rated bond class, Standard & Poor's assumes a foreclosure rate of 15% with a 43% loss severity (34.5% market value decline and 25% foreclosure costs on loans with a 12% or lower mortgage rate). Given these conditions, the required loss coverage for a triple-A rating is 6.5%, the product of multiplying foreclosure rate with loss severity.

Considerations of Characteristics of the Underlying Mortgages

One unique aspect of private-label securities is the wide difference in the characteristics of their underlying mortgage pools. They differ in terms of the size of the original loan balance and mortgage rate. More important, the mortgage pools differ in LTV, geographic dispersion of the underlying properties, maturity term of mortgages (30-year versus 15-year or balloons, fixed-rate versus adjustable-rate) type of mortgages (single-family versus planned unit development "PUD," townhouse, condominium, cooperative apartment), tenure (owner-occupied, vacation home, or rental property), purpose (purchase money versus refinancing or relocation), and credit quality of mortgagors ("A" quality versus "B," "C," or "D"). Also, mortgage pools vary in the completeness of mortgage documentation. Each of these characteristics has a different risk implication.

For example, for a triple-A rating, DCR believes that ARMs are 28% more risky but 15-year FRMs are 50% less risky than 30-year FRMs. Mortgages with a 10% interest rate are 17% more risky than those with an 8% rate. Renter-occupied properties are 90% more risky than owner-occupied. All in all, the benchmark mortgage pool has the following features: 30-year fixed-rate single-family purchase-money mortgages with an 8% average mortgage rate, a 75% LTV, owner-occupied, full documentation, and "A" quality borrowers. For a triple-A rating, DCR assumes an 11.25% cumulative *loss incidence* and a 40.4% weighted average loss severity. Thus the loss coverage is 4.54% (11.25% × 40.4%).

It is significant to note the high credit worthiness of relocation mortgages ("relos"). Relos are 20% less risky than comparable purchase money mortgages. They are originated for transferred corporate employees (transferees), who are generally members of middle- to high-level management. Corporations that have extensive relocation programs are mostly Fortune 500 companies. They usually work with mortgage lenders with a national origination network and quality mortgage underwriting standards to provide efficient financial assistance to transferees. While data on relos are not readily available, it is believed that they are small relative to total originations but significant among non-conforming originations. NSCOR 1996-6 is backed exclusively by relos.

Recent surveys of relocation programs of major corporations have revealed that the average stay of transferees is around four years. Based on this average, relos would have an expected average life of even less than five years. Relos prepay slightly slower than non-relos in the initial years, but substantially faster than non-relos in later years. (This feature explains the PPC pricing of NSCOR 1996-6.) Corporations are unlikely to move the same transferees again within the first two years. But after a few years, transferees normally will be moved again for reasons of promotion or changing assignments. Surveys suggest that transferees on average experience more than four transfers during their careers. The high cost of transfers slows the prepayment speed in initial years, but the frequency of career changes accelerates it in later years.

Considerations of the Quality of the Issuer/Primary Servicer and the Master Service

The quality of a mortgage pool is not solely a function of its own characteristics. It also depends critically on the quality of the operations and procedures of its issuer/primary servicer and master servicer of the pool. The quality considerations are critically important for private-label securities because of the high concentration of issuers. As shown in Exhibit 5, the top five issuers have accounted for 65% of the $30 billion of private-label securities issued in the first nine months of 1996. The market share for the top 10 issuers has been a stunning 85%. The quality of their operations represents that of the industry.

According to Fitch, the main function of the issuer/primary servicer and master servicer is to protect the value of the pool and to ensure the timely pass-through of the interest and principal payment from the underlying mortgagors to the security investors. From Fitch's point of view, the issuer/primary servicer performs three major functions: (1) collection and pass-through of funds, including collections/workout, timely remittances, investor accounting, custodial accounting management, (2) collateral protection, including foreclosures/bankruptcies, real estate owned management, escrow management, and (3) servicing quality control. How these three functions are carried out has an important bearing on the credit performance of a mortgage pool and eventually the credit quality of the security backed by the pool.

Exhibit 5: Issuance Volume and Market Share of Top Ten Issuers of Private-Label Securities
First Nine Months, 1996

Issuer	Issuance Volume ($ million)	Market Share (%)
Residential Funding Corp.	8,755	28.9
GE Capital Mortgage Services	4,335	14.3
Independent National Mortgage	2,496	8.2
Merit Securities	2,095	6.9
Norwest Asset Mortgage Corp.	2,068	6.8
Prudential Home Mortgage	1,951	6.4
Merrill Lynch	1,223	4.0
Donaldson Lufkin & Jenrette	953	3.1
Salomon Brothers	913	3.0
Bear Stearns Mortgage Sec. Corp.	833	2.8
All others	4,706	15.5

Source: Reprinted with permission of Inside Mortgage Securities, Copyright 1996, Bethesda, Maryland.
(301-951-1240)

To the extent that a mortgage pool consists of originations from several primary servicers, a master servicer is designated. In this case, the quality of its master servicer is also crucial to the credit rating of a security. The master servicer tracks its primary servicers in many aspects just like primary servicers track their mortgagors. Most important, the master servicer ensures that monthly mortgage cash flows from primary servicers are accurately collected and timely forwarded to investors. The master servicer also monitors the overall status of mortgages of each primary servicer in terms of mortgage insurance status, delinquencies, defaults, and foreclosures.

LOSS EXPERIENCE

One striking quality of triple-A rate private-label securities issued since the late 1970s is that they have experienced virtually no losses. In fact, for those backed by fixed-rate mortgages, there have been absolutely no losses. Given the generous provision of loss coverage and the overall sound economic conditions over the past decade, it is understandable that triple-A rated classes would have such an excellent record of credit performance.

The excellent performance of private-label securities was identified in a June 1995 study by Standard & Poor's. It first examined 610 publicly rated 30-year fixed-rate private-label securities issued from the late 1970s through mid-1994. The study found that the average cumulative loss as a percent of original pool balance ranged between as low as 0.1% for 1993 issues to 1.15% of 1988 issues. The 1993 issues had a low loss average because of their relatively young age. By contrast, the high loss average of the 1988 issues can be explained by the fact that losses tend to rise as pools age (for this reason, 1994 issues thus far have had no losses). The losses tend to peak in the 7th to the 10th year. (As will be shown later, this experience provides the base for formulating the *standard default assumption of PSA.*) Also, a significant portion of private-label securities are backed by mortgages originated in California. The relative high loss average for the 1988 issues reflected the particularly depressed California housing market during the mild national economic recession in the early 1990s.

Since even the highest loss average was substantially below the provision of loss coverage, none of the triple-A rated classes ever experienced a loss. In fact, neither did double- and single-A classes suffer any losses. The study also examined the loss experience of 151 securities backed by 15-year fixed-rate mortgages. There, the performance was even more impressive. The percentage of average losses ranged between 0.02% in 1993 and 0.35% in 1988. Even the subordinated BBB- and BB-rated classes experienced no losses. (Many issues originally did not have "deeply credit tranched" classes. Thus, the losses were derived hypothetically from credit tranching these classes using the current rating criteria.) In general, because of substantially shorter amortization period, 15-year securities have much lower losses than 30-year mortgage backed securities.

The Standard & Poor's study also looked into the loss experience of 132 securities backed by ARMs. As expected, the losses were substantially higher for ARMs than FRMs. It stands to reason that ARMs are more risky than FRMs because their upward adjustment in payments in the midst of rising interest rates creates more onerous financial burden for mortgagors than FRMs. Additionally, most of the ARMs backing private-label securities were originated in California. The housing recession in the early 1990s accentuated mortgage defaults of ARMs. The study showed that even triple-A classes suffered a loss of 0.34% in 1988.

The excellent credit performance of the senior class was also verified in a May 1996 study by Moody's. Based on its database of over 1,700 transactions issued between 1987 and 1995 with original balances totaling more than $320 billion, Moody's found that the average cumulative loss rate as of March 1996 was 0.54%. Again, the loss rate varied considerably by issuance year. The 1989 transactions have a high cumulative loss rate of 2.11%, whereas those of the 1987 and 1991 transactions were only 1.32% and 0.79%, respectively. Still, these losses were substantially below the loss coverage allowed for triple-A rated classes.

THE IMPORTANCE OF HOUSE PRICE APPRECIATION

While the innovative credit enhancement mechanism has ensured an impeccable credit performance for private-label securities, house price appreciation has played an important role in sustaining their credit quality. In fact, the bottom line of the credit of a private-label security is the size of the accumulated principal loss of the mortgage pool. As discussed above, this loss depends critically on the loss severity, which is a function of the liquidating value of the house. The liquidating value is ultimately determined by house price appreciation (or depreciation).

Empirically, during periods of rapid house price appreciation, mortgages tend to have a low incidence of default. Further, given the inevitability of defaults of a given mortgage pool, a modest house price appreciation can comfortably cover the bulk of foreclosure costs and limit the potential principal loss. During the past 10 years of the existence of private-label securities, house prices have in general appreciated significantly. The simple fact that house prices have appreciated at all has greatly limited the accumulated principal losses of mortgage pools.

The National Experience

Over the past 25 years, the monthly annualized change in house prices, measured as the percent change in the sales-weighted median prices of new and existing homes, has almost always been positive (1991 was the only exception). It has ranged between −1.6% and 16.5% (see Exhibit 6). During the 1970s, when both housing demand and inflation were historically strong, the annual nominal house price appreciation averaged about 10%. Adjusted for inflation, the average of annual appreciation "in real terms" still amounted to more than 3%. As demand weakened moderately and the economy suffered a severe recession during the early part of the decade, the average of annual nominal appreciation in the 1980s literally halved with virtually no real appreciation. Similarly, the 1990s also started with a housing recession, and nominal house prices declined significantly. In recent years, however, the housing market has rebounded with a vengeance and the annual nominal and real house price appreciation has averaged over 5% and 2%, respectively.

This 25-year history suggests that house price appreciation is a function of the health of the nation's economy and the strength of the housing market. With rare exceptions, only during periods of economic recession and/or slowdown in housing activity, such as in 1974-74, 1981-82, and 1990-92, have annual nominal house prices risen by less than 3% with negative real appreciation. In non-recessionary years, the nominal appreciation has been mostly above 3% with a positive real appreciation. Going forward, house prices are expected to keep pace with inflation. In fact, as the economy maintains strength and the housing market remains robust, house prices should appreciate slightly faster than inflation. Given a 3% generally expected annual inflation for the next few years, even without any real increases, the nominal house prices should appreciate at least 3% annually.

The California Experience

While national economic conditions affect the change in house prices, the idiosyncrasy of the regional economy has a more direct bearing on local house prices. This aspect is important in private-label securities, as the majority of their underlying mortgages are often concentrated in a limited number of states. More significant, over one-third of private-label securities are backed by mortgages originated in California.

Exhibit 6: Monthly Nominal and Real House Price Appreciation, January 1970 - August 1996

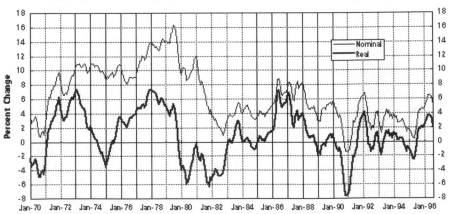

Source: BLOOMBERG Financial Markets

Exhibit 7: Annualized Changes in House Prices by Quarter in U.S. versus California, 1980:1 to 1996:1

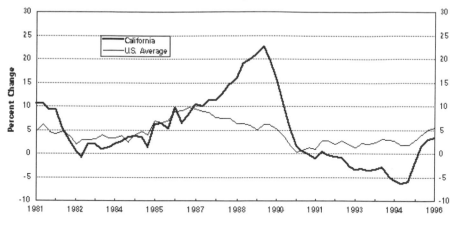

Source: OFHEO (Office of Federal Housing Oversight) House Price Indexes

For the past 15 years, house prices in California have moved in a similar though exaggerated pattern to that of the nation. Exhibit 7 shows that the annual changes in its house prices fluctuated between 26% and −6%, far more volatile than those of the national experience. The most volatile period occurred in the late 1980s, when the California housing market experienced a severe recession. While it has lasted longer in California than most other states, the recession appears to have ended in 1994-95. House prices have begun to appreciate more significantly, though still modestly behind the national average. For the next few years, the outlook for California house prices is encouraging. Its economy has shown strong growth in the past year with significant expansion in employment in the telecommunications, technology, computer, and film industries. A robust economic recovery will have a healthy impact on California's house price appreciation, ultimately ensuring the high credit quality of private-label securities.

PREPAYMENT PATTERN

Like their agency-guaranteed counterparts, prepayments of private-label securities are influenced by refinancing and housing activity. However, because the characteristics of non-conforming mortgage pools are not as uniform as those of conforming mortgages, prepayments of private-label securities tend to be more volatile than those of agency-guaranteed securities. Most significant, the servicing spread — that is the difference between the gross weighted average mortgage rate of the underlying pool (gross WAC) and the net weighted average coupon rate of the security (net WAC) — varies considerably among the numerous issuers of private-label securities. Additionally, there are wide differences among pools in terms of the size of loans, LTV, geographic concentration of underlying properties, tenure (owner-occupied versus rental property), and credit quality of mortgagors ("A" quality versus "B," "C," or "D"). All these contribute to the unique prepayment pattern of private-label securities.

Generally speaking, private-label securities prepay substantially faster than comparable-coupon agency-guaranteed securities in a declining interest rate environment. Because of the larger loan balance, non-conforming mortgagors are in higher income brackets than their conforming counterparts. Non-conforming mortgagors are therefore financially more capable of taking advantage of declines in interest rates to refinance. Further, they tend to move more frequently for reasons of upgrading housing accommodations and changing jobs. All these result in private-label securities' faster prepayments than agency-guaranteed securities.

Prepayments of Selected Transactions

To compare the prepayment patterns of private-label and agency-guaranteed securities, Exhibits 8, 9, and 10 present prepayments of selected issues of Prudential Home Mortgage Securities (Bloomberg Ticker: PHMS), GE Capital Mortgage Services, Inc. (GECMS), and Residential Funding Mortgage Securities (RFMS) along with selected issues of FNMA REMICs (FNR). These securities are selected on the basis of large original balance, similar issuance date, and comparable gross WAC. Prepayments of private-label securities are paired into three groups to compare separately with FNMA REMICs with an 8%, 8.5%%, and 9% gross WAC.

All selected securities experienced sharp acceleration of prepayments in the initial years because they were issued either just before or in the midst of the huge refinancing wave of 1992-94. The significant and consistent difference between all selected private-label and agency-guaranteed securities was the much faster prepayment speeds of the former than the latter. It reflected the acute sensitivity to declining mortgage rates on the part of non-conforming mortgagors. By the same token, as mortgage rates rose, prepayments of private-label securities also dropped more sharply than agency-guaranteed securities. For example, prepayments of GECMS 1993-5A with an 8% WAC soared to nearly 3200% PSA in late 1993. This speed was more than twice as fast as those of FNR 1993-4 with an 8.1% WAC. However, as mortgage rates heightened close to 9% in late 1994, prepayments of both securities plunged to just around 100% PSA.

Housing Turnover Rate

Between late 1994 and 1996, as mortgage rates fluctuated between 7.5% and 8.5%, all prepayments oscillated between 150% and 250% PSA. This pattern is particularly clear when prepayment rates of all selected private-label securities are expressed in 12-month moving averages. The bulk of the narrow range of prepayments can be explained by the housing turnover rate — a ratio of existing home sales to the stock of occupied single-family houses. As discussed in Chapter

4, the turnover rate can be expressed in terms of PSA speeds. In 1995, for example, annual existing home sales totaled 3.8 million units and the housing stock was estimated at 63.7 million. The housing turnover rate therefore was right around 6%, or 100% PSA. The incremental speeds over the housing turnover rate can be attributed to defaults, refinancing to ARMs or shorter maturity mortgages with lower initial rates, curtailments, and miscellaneous factors, such as fire, flood, death, etc.

Exhibit 8: Prepayments of Selected Prudential Home Mortgage Securities Issues in 1992

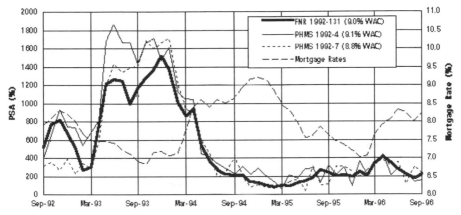

Source: BLOOMBERG Financial Markets

Exhibit 8A: Prepayments of Selected Prudential Home Mortgage Securities Issues — One Year Moving Average

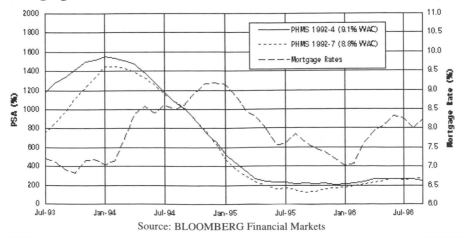

Source: BLOOMBERG Financial Markets

Exhibit 9: Prepayments of Selected GE Capital Mortgage Securities Issues in 1993

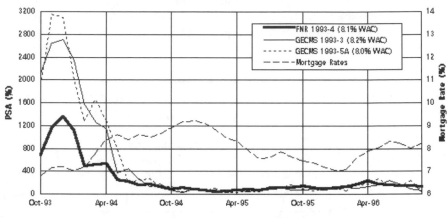

Source: BLOOMBERG Financial Markets

Exhibit 9A: Prepayments of Selected GE Capital Mortgage Securities Issues in 1993 — One Year Moving Average

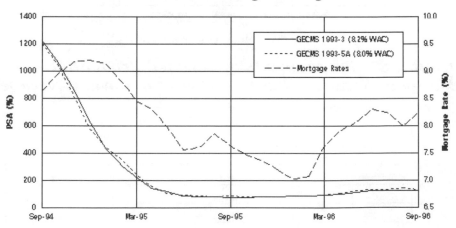

Source: BLOOMBERG Financial Markets

Exhibit 10: Prepayments of Selected Residential Funding Mortgage Securities Issues in 1992

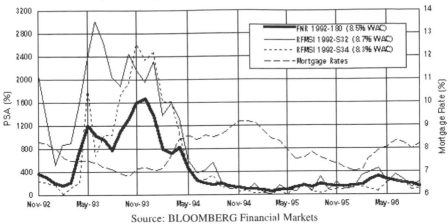

Source: BLOOMBERG Financial Markets

Exhibit 10A: Prepayments of Selected Residential Funding Mortgage Securities Issues — One Year Moving Average

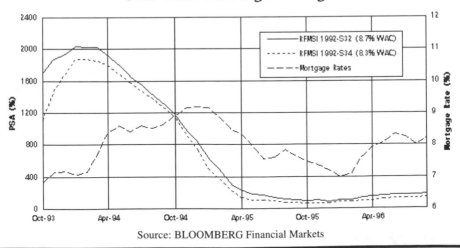

Source: BLOOMBERG Financial Markets

Incidence of Default

Defaults are not a significant factor of prepayments of private-label securities. As mentioned earlier, an October 1996 study by Morgan Stanley indicated that non-conforming loans have had consistently lower delinquency rates than conventional mortgages as reported by the Mortgage Bankers Association of America. The bulk of conventional mortgages reported by MBA are conforming loans. By studying the total delinquency rates (defined as the sum of 30-, 60-, and 90-day delinquencies plus foreclosures and real estate owned) of 1994 and 1995 of non-conforming loans originated by 10 of the largest issuers of private-label securities, Morgan Stanley found the delinquency rates of non-conforming loans have been between 0.2% and 0.6% lower than conforming loans. For September 1996, the delinquency rates of the two types of mortgages were 2.44% and 2.84%, respectively. Since non-conforming loans have a lower delinquency rate, it stands to reason that they have a lower default rate than conforming loans.

The Standard Default Assumption

While non-conforming loans have relatively low defaults, investors still are interested in tracking their performance in conjunction with the evaluation of prepayments. This is particularly true in the cases of subordinated classes, whose cash flows are critically dependent on the default experience of non-conforming loans. For that purpose, the Public Securities Association promulgated a standard default assumption (SDA) for the analysis of mortgage defaults and the projection of monthly mortgage cash flows. Conceptually, the SDA curve is similar to that of the PSA curve in prepayments. A "100% SDA" is defined as the incidence of default of a 30-year mortgage pool conforming to the following pattern (Exhibit 11):

1. An annualized default rate of 0.02% in the first month;
2. The default rate rises by an annualized rate of 0.02% per month from months 1 to 30;
3. The default rate peaks at 0.6% and remains so between months 30 and 60,
4. From months 61 to 120, the default rate declines linearly by an annualized rate of 0.0095% per month from the peak rate of 0.6% to 0.03% in month 120;

Exhibit 11: PSA's Standard Default Assumption (SDA) Curve

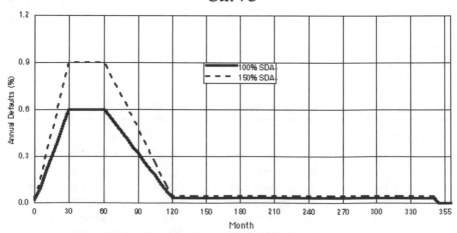

Source: Public Securities Association

5. The default rate stabilizes at 0.03% from month 121 to 348 (this assumes a liquidation period of 12 months to dispose properties and recover loan loss; if however the liquidation period is shorter than 12 month, then the 0.03% rate will last longer); and, finally

6. During the final year of the mortgage pool, the default rate drops to 0%.

In pricing private-label securities, however, market participants may or may not use the SDA curve explicitly. For example, some investors may assume a 130% PSA and 150% SDA to price a current-coupon private-label security. For the same security, other investors may simply incorporate the SDA into a 150% PSA assumption to evaluate the price/yield and the average life of the security.

PRICING AND TRADING

Despite their excellent record of credit performance, private-label securities have been priced to yield more than agency-guaranteed securities. In the minds of investors, a triple-A credit is after all not an "agency" credit. In fact, for many investors, mutual funds in particular, private-label securities are not eligible investments because they are not classified as "government-guaranteed" securities. The lack of large investor base therefore result in higher yields of private-label securities.

In addition to perceived credit quality differences, private-label securities also trade "behind" agency-guaranteed securities for three reasons. First, because of the relatively faster and volatile prepayments, private-label securities are viewed as having a greater prepayment risk than comparable-coupon agency-guaranteed securities. As compensation for a greater prepayment risk, private-label securities are required to provide higher yields. Second, for risk-adjusted capital requirements of commercial banks, private-label securities have a risk weight of 50%. By comparison, the risk weight is 20% for Fannie Mae- and Freddie Mac-guaranteed securities; 0% for Ginnie Mae-guaranteed securities. As a result, commercial banks demand higher yields to make up for setting aside a greater amount of capital for holding private-label securities. Third, if private-label securities are purchased on a financed basis, they are subject to higher costs of financing in terms of interest charges and "haircuts." (The haircut is the discount of the value of the collateral for purposes of borrowing.)

One additional reason for the yield difference is the treatment of *compensating interest*. This aspect is unique only among certain private-label securities. Compensating interest is a payment by the security issuer to investors to cover the interest shortfall as a result of mortgage prepayment. When mortgagors prepay, they will pay off the remaining loan balance plus the accrued interest between the beginning of the month and the time they prepay. However, for investors, a full coupon payment for the month is expected. Thus, there is an interest shortfall between the time of prepayment and the end of the month. Some private-label securities issuers have reserve funds to cover the shortfall; some do not. (For agency-guaranteed securities, all seller/servicers uniformly cover the shortfall.)

Exhibit 12: Yield Spreads of Selected Tranches of Agency-Guaranteed and Triple-A Rated Private-Label REMICs, As of October 25, 1996

Average Life	PACs (basis point)		Sequentials (basis point)	
(year)	Agency	Private	Agency	Private
2	36	51	70	95
3	38	54	80	105
5	44	60	85	110
7	65	80	95	120
10	68	83	100	125
20	72	90	105	130

Note: Yield spreads are indications of bids. Underlying collateral for all REMICs are generic new production 30-year 7s.

Source: Oppenheimer & Co., Inc.

To the extent that private-label securities do not provide compensating interest, their yields would have to be higher than those that do. The yield difference between the two is dependent on prepayment speeds and the expected average lives of the securities at offering pricing speeds. A DCR study indicated that for short average live tranches, the difference is minimal. However, for tranches with original average lives of 20 years under an accelerated prepayment speed of 1500% PSA, the difference could be as much as 24 basis points.

For the above reasons, private-label securities are priced and traded between 15 and 25 basis points higher in yields than comparable agency-guaranteed securities. Exhibit 12 shows the yield spread differences (bid side) between agency-guaranteed and private-label securities by average life and type of maturity tranche. The yield spread differences actually have narrowed significantly in 1996. In the beginning of 1996, they ranged between 25 to 40 basis points. This narrowing has been primary the result of investors recognizing the consistently high credit quality and attractive yields of private-label securities.

Chapter 9

Analysis of Dollar Rolls

- The Significance of the Forward Market
- Selling the Roll versus Continuing to Hold
- The Accretion of the Forward Price

THE SIGNIFICANCE OF THE FORWARD MARKET

As mentioned in Chapter 3, the forward market is unique for mortgage-backed securities. It exists because originating mortgages and pooling them for the issuance of mortgage-backed securities is a time consuming process. It normally takes up to four months from the time home buyers submit loan applications to the origination of mortgages and finally the issuance of securities. To secure future delivery prices at present market interest rates, mortgage lenders need to sell their production forward. Thus, the forward market shelters the lenders from the unknown of future interest rates by allowing them to deliver to-be-originated mortgages at prices determined by current market conditions for at least one-month forward. The forward settlement is a vitally important means of hedging for lenders in the primary mortgage market.

The forward market is also uniquely useful for mortgage investors. This usefulness is derived from the price difference between the cash and the forward markets. As pointed out in Chapter 5, the price of a mortgage security reflects the present value of its future cash flow. The difference between a "cash price" and a "forward price" — colloquially termed the "drop" — is therefore the difference in the time value of the two settlement periods. For current coupon mortgage securities, the drop is always positive (in a positively sloped yield curve environment), meaning that the cash price is higher than the forward price. Investors may take advantage of this difference by selling their holdings of mortgage securities in the cash market and buying them back in the forward market. By doing so, investors get to use the selling proceeds for the time period between the cash and forward settlement dates. This transaction is called a *dollar roll*, a special term in the mortgage securities market.

SELLING THE ROLL VERSUS CONTINUING TO HOLD

A dollar roll entails a portfolio manager selling a mortgage security (to a buyer who is most likely a security dealer) for cash settlement and simultaneously buying back *substantially the same* security for forward settlement. Typically, the roll period between the cash and the forward settlement dates can be as long as four months. In trading jargon, selling cash and buying forward is called "selling the roll." Conversely, buying cash and selling forward is "buying the roll." For agency-guaranteed securities of all coupons, there is a calendar of dollar roll settlement dates published by the Public Securities Association. For example, a 1996 November/December (hereafter, Nov/Dec) dollar roll of GNMA 7.5s settles on 11/19/96 and 12/18/96, respectively.[1]

The definition of "substantially the same" security is important in the accounting treatment for dollar rolls. To conform to the accounting definition of "substantially the same," a security must (1) be backed by similar mortgages — basically those that are secured by single-family houses, (2) guaranteed by the same agency, (3) carry the same coupon rate and original stated maturity, and (4) meet the "good delivery" requirement, currently 1.0% of the variance of principal balance originally delivered.

Additionally, for a dollar roll to qualify as a "financing" transaction for regulatory purposes, as opposed to an "asset sale," which requires booking any gains or losses for the transaction, the seller must have owned the securities for at least 35 days before entering the dollar roll transaction. Further, there is a regulatory requirement for savings and loan associations (thrifts) to "take delivery" of roll transactions within 12 months. Non-thrifts, however, can do dollar rolls without ever taking deliveries.

By selling the roll, the portfolio manager gets use of the sale proceeds for the roll period. *During the roll period, however, the manager gives up the monthly principal and interest cash flow of the rolled security.* At the end of the roll period, the manager unwinds the financing by buying back the security at the lower, predetermined forward price. Thus, the fundamental difference between dollar roll and *collateralized borrowing* is the ownership of the interim cash flow of principal and interest. It is given up by the dollar roll seller, but not the collateralized borrower.

Numerical Example

Using new production 30-year GNMA 7.5s (hereafter, GNMA 7.5s) as an example, Exhibit 1 illustrates the arbitrage of selling the Nov/Dec roll. The example assumes that GNMA 7.5s with a WAM of 353 months trade at a cash price (November) of $100^{10}/_{32}$ and at a forward price (December) of 100. It further assumes a 5.25% short-term reinvestment rate (the alternative short-term financing rate) and a prepayment rate of 130% PSA in November.

Facing these market conditions for GNMA 7.5s, a portfolio manager has two alternatives: (1) arbitrage with the Nov/Dec price difference by selling the roll or (2) simply hold on to the security in the portfolio. By selling the roll of $1 million principal of GNMA 7.5s at a cash price of $100^{10}/_{32}$ for 11/19/96 settle-

---

[1] On Bloomberg screens, for settlement dates of GNMA 7.5s, type GNSF7.5 <MTGE> <GO>, and then type <MSD>.

ment, the manager can reinvest the proceeds for 29 days (11 days in November and 18 in December) between the cash and the forward settlement dates. By continuing to hold, the manager simply "marks to market" GNMA 7.5s at a forward price of 100 on the settlement date of December 18.

The proceeds of selling the roll, as shown in Exhibit 1, are $1,006,875 (Item S3). This amount is the sum of the dollar value of GNMA 7.5s at the cash price, $1,003,125 (S1) and 18 days of accrued interest, $3,750 (S2), between November 1 and 18. By comparison, at the end of the roll period, on December 18, the manager in effect pays back $1,001,077.82 (C3). This amount is the sum of the value of GNMA 7.5s with remaining principal at the forward price of 100 (C1) and 17 days of accrued interest of $3,532.97 (C2) between December 1 and 18.

Exhibit 1: An Hypothetical Example of Selling the Roll versus Continuing to Hold, New Production 30-Year GNMA 7.5s with a WAM of 353 Months

	Selling the Roll		Continuing to Hold
S1	Dollar value of principal on 11/19/96 at a price of $100^{10}/_{32}$: = $1,000,000 \times 1.003125$ = $1,003,125.00	C1	Remaining principal on 12/18/96 at a price of 100: = $997,544.85
S2	Accrued interest of 18 days: = $1,000,000 \times (0.075/12) \times (18/30)$ = $3,750.00	C2	Accrued interest for 17 days: = $1,000,000 \times (0.075/12) \times (17/30)$ = $3,532.97
S3	Proceeds of selling the roll (S1 + S2): =$1,003,125.00 + $3,750.00 =$1,006,875.00	C3	Dollar value of principal plus accrued interest (C1 +C2): = $997,544.85 + $3,532.97 = $1,001,077.82
S4	Reinvestment of proceeds for 29 days at an annual rate of 5.25%: = $1,006,875.00 \times (0.0525/12) \times (29/30)$ = $4,258.24	C4	Scheduled amortization in November: = $706.49
		C5	Prepayment at a 130% PSA in November: = $1,752.47
		C6	Coupon income for November: = $1,000,000 \times (0.075/12)$ = $6,250
		C7	Interim cash flow of November: (C4 + C5 + C6) = $706.49 + $1,752.47 + $6,250 = $8,708.96
S5	Total future value of selling the roll (S3 + S4): = $1,003,125 +$3,750 + $4, 258.24 = $1,011,133.24	C8	Total future value of continuing to hold (C3 + C7): = $1,001,077.82 + $8,708.96 = $1,009,786.78

Arbitrage Advantage of Selling the Roll (S5 – C8):
= $1,011,133.24 – $1,009,786.78 = $1,346.46

Source: BLOOMBERG Financial Markets.

It appears that the above difference already points to an advantage of selling the roll. But that is only a partial analysis. A total evaluation of selling the roll versus continuing to hold should cover the aspects of reinvestment from the proceeds of selling the roll and the give-up of the interim interest and principal cash flow during the roll period. Thus, a complete evaluation should compare the future value of the two alternatives.

Exhibit 1 shows that the future value of selling the roll is $1,011,133.24. It consists of the November sale proceeds of GNMA 7.5s, $1,006,875 (S3), and the reinvestment of these proceeds at a short-term rate of 5.25% for 29 days, $4,258.24 (S4). Alternatively, the future value of continuing to hold is $1,009,786.78 (C8), which is the sum of the December value of GNMA 7.5s, $1,001,077.82 (C3) plus the ownership of the interim interest and principal cash flow of $8,708.96 (C7). The interim cash flow consists of three components: amortized principal in November, $706.49 (C4); prepaid principal, $1,752.47 (C5); and, coupon income, $6,250 (C6).

By comparing the two future values, it is clear that selling the roll is a more attractive alternative with an arbitrage advantage of $1,346.46 per $1 million original principal. If, however, both alternatives were to have more or less the same future value, the manager will be indifferent because there is no arbitrage opportunity.

Attractive Source of Short-Term Financing

Selling the roll is an effective way for the portfolio manager to secure short-term financing. It can be viewed that, by selling the roll, the manager borrows the sale proceeds of $1,006,875 for 29-days and pays back $1,009,786.78, the future value of continuing to hold the security, at the forward settlement date. The *implied financing rate* (IFR) therefore can be calculated as follows:

$$\text{IFR} = [(\text{future value of continuing to hold} / \text{proceeds of selling the roll}) - 1] \times (360/29)$$
$$= (1,009,786.78/1,006,875 - 1) \times 360/29$$
$$= 3.59\%$$

The implied financing rate can also be approximated by taking the difference between the short-term reinvestment rate and the roll's *arbitrage advantage rate* (AAR). The AAR can be expressed by the following formula:

$$\text{AAR} = [(\text{future value of selling-the-roll} - \text{future value of continuing-to-hold})/\text{future value of continuing-to-hold}] \times 360/29$$
$$= [(1,011,133.24 - 1,009,786.78)/1,009,786.78] \times 360/29$$
$$= 1.65\%$$

Since the alternative short-term financing rate is 5.25% and the arbitrage advantage rate is 1.65%, it implies that the financing rate of selling the roll is 5.25% − 1.65% = 3.6%. This rate is very close to the implied financing rate first calculated.

Exhibit 2: One-Month Drop and Implied Financing Rate for New Production 30-Year GNMA 7.5s at a Cash Price of 100¹⁰⁄₃₂

Drop (tick)	0	4	6	8	10	12	16	20
Implied Financing Rate (%)	7.44	5.90	5.13	4.36	3.59	2.82	1.28	−0.25

Note: All coupons are assumed to have a WAM of 353 months with a one-month prepayment speed of 130% PSA. Interim reinvestment rate is 5.25%

Source: BLOOMBERG Financial Markets.

The Drop and Break-Even Drop

The above example shows that the arbitrage of selling the roll represents an attractive source of short-term financing. This arbitrage exists primarily because of the size of the drop. That is, the forward price is significantly lower than the cash price. Given the size of the drop, the implied financing rate is mathematically determined by the coupon rate of the mortgage pass-through and the monthly prepayment rate during the roll period. Furthermore, perhaps more important, supply and demand conditions in the cash and forward markets can significantly increase or decrease the size of the drop.

Given the price and the coupon rate of a mortgage security along with its interim prepayment rate and the reinvestment rate, there is a corresponding implied financing rate for each drop. The size of the drop and the implied financing rate are inversely related: as the drop increases, the implied financing rate declines.

Continuing the numerical example above, Exhibit 2 shows that if the drop increases from 10 ticks to 16 ticks (a 99²⁶⁄₃₂ forward price), the implied financing rate of selling the roll declines by 231 basis points to 1.28%. A further increase of the drop to 20 ticks will reduce the financing cost to negative. This implies that the security holder is actually being paid to borrow! Of course, this rarely happens.

But, in the early 1990s, when the REMIC market was exceedingly robust with dealers constantly looking for current-coupon pass-throughs in the cash market to close transactions of newly issued REMICs, cash prices heightened far above the forward price. As a result, the drop enlarged to levels that virtually had a zero implied financing rate. Conversely, if the drop shrinks to zero — that is the forward price is the same as the cash price — the implied financing rate would surge to 7.44%, far greater than the alternative financing rate of 5.25%. This, of course, would never happen because investors will simply go elsewhere to borrow at a short-term rate of 5.25%.

Exhibit 2 also shows that at a drop of 6 ticks, the implied financing rate of GNMA 7.5s is 5.13%, only slightly lower than the 5.25% of alternative short-term financing rate. *When the drop is such that the implied financing rate is identical to the short-term financing rate, it is called the "break-even" drop.* At this drop, the security holder would be indifferent between selling the roll or continuing to hold the security.

Exhibit 3: Implied Financing Rates under Various Cash Prices and Drops for Selected Coupons of 30-Year GNMAs

Coupon	Cash Price	Break-Even	Drop (tick)					
(%)	(32 nds)	Drop (tick)	0	4	6	8	10	12
6.0	92-28	3.5	6.65%	4.99%	4.16%	3.33%	2.50%	1.67%
7.0	97-28	5.0	7.18	5.61	4.82	4.04	3.25	2.46
7.5	100-10	6.0	7.43	5.90	5.13	4.36	3.59	2.82
8.0	102-24	6.5	7.67	6.17	5.42	4.67	3.92	3.17
9.0	105-20	8.0	8.33	6.87	6.14	5.41	4.68	3.95

Note: All coupons are assumed to have a WAM of 353 months with a one-month prepayment speed of 130% PSA. Interim reinvestment rate is 5.25%

Source: BLOOMBERG Financial Markets.

Exhibit 4: Implied Financing Rates Given Cash Prices, a 4-Tick Drop and Prepayment Rates for Selected Coupons of GNMAs

Coupon	Cash Price	Prepayment Rate (% PSA)					
(%)	(32 nds)	100	150	200	250	300	400
6.0	92-28	2.50%	2.56%	2.63%	2.69%	2.76%	2.90%
7.0	97-28	3.24	3.26	3.28	3.29	3.31	3.35
7.5	100-10	3.59	3.59	3.59	3.58	3.58	3.58
8.0	102-24	3.93	3.91	3.89	3.86	3.84	3.79
9.0	105-20	4.71	4.66	4.62	4.57	4.52	4.43

Note: All coupons are assumed to have a WAM of 353 months. Interim reinvestment rate is 5.25%.
Source: BLOOMBERG Financial Markets.

The size of the break-even drop varies from coupon to coupon at different price levels. It is, however, positively associated with the coupon rate. Assuming all coupons prepay at a 130% PSA with a WAM of 353 months, Exhibit 3 shows that the break-even drop for 30-year GNMA 6s at a cash price of $92^{28}/_{32}$ is 3.5 ticks. At specific prices for GNMA 7s, 8s, and 9s, their break-even drops increase steadily to 5, 6.5, and 8 ticks, respectively. Exhibit 3 also shows that given the size of the drop, the implied financing rate is lower for lower coupons. For GNMA 6s, a 6-tick drop has an implied financing rate of 4.16%. The same drop for GNMA 9s has an implied financing rate of 6.14%.

Interim Prepayment Rate

The interim prepayment rate can also significantly influence the implied financing rate. The influence is felt at the end of the roll period when the borrower has to buy back the remaining principal. Exhibit 4 shows the implied financing rates of selected coupons of 30-year GNMAs, given a 4-tick drop, under various prepayment rates. *For discount coupons, the implied financing rate rises with the interim prepayment rate.* It stands to reason that prepayments enhance the yield of discount coupons. To give up this positive factor during the roll period increases the implied financing rate for the borrower. By contrast, *for premium coupons, the financing rate declines with the interim prepayment rate.* Since prepayments reduce the yield of premium coupons, the give-up of interim cash flow for the roll period reduces the implied financing cost for the borrower. Thus, in an environment of declining interest rates with accelerating prepayments, the buyer of the premium-coupon roll has to be aware of the implicit prepayment risk.

The Drop and Cash-Forward Market Dynamics

The dynamics of supply and demand is the main reason that the drop actually traded in the dollar roll market can be significantly greater than the break-even drop. Most important, the supply of current-coupon mortgage pass-throughs in the forward market is dominated by loan originations in the primary mortgage market. As mentioned at the outset, the mortgage securities market is unique in its forward delivery mechanism. The forward delivery facilitates the sale of to-be-originated mortgages at prices determined at current market interest rates. These sales constitute the major supply of forward deliveries. In 1992-93, when rampant refinancing coupled with strong housing recovery ballooned mortgage originations to almost $1 trillion annually, the forward market expanded dramatically.

On the other hand, there are often strong demands for securities in the cash market when dealers need to cover their short cash positions. As was just mentioned, this often was the case in the early 1990s. To underwrite REMICs, dealers were constantly on the lookout for WAM-specific mortgage current-coupon pass-throughs in the cash market to satisfy the closing of REMICs. Since dealers need only to deliver back "substantially the same" securities in the forward market, dollar rolls were extremely useful for REMIC underwriting. Meanwhile, by offsetting the purchase of pass-throughs in the cash market, the dealers also significantly increased the supply of pass-throughs in the forward market.

THE ACCRETION OF THE FORWARD PRICE

If interest rates and market conditions remain unchanged, the forward price will elevate gradually through time in a mathematical way to the level of the cash price. Again, in the previous numerical example, when 12/18/96 becomes the cash settlement date, the original forward settlement price of 100 for GNMA 7.5s will rise and become the cash price, precisely $100^{10}/_{32}$. Market dynamics aside, the mathematics behind this difference is simply the importance of coupon income versus the financing cost during the roll period. The cash price contains a 1-month coupon income at 7.5% with a 1-month financing cost of the position at 5.25%. By contrast, the forward price includes no coupon income and no financing cost. But, in terms of total outlay, the cash price should equal the forward price.

To illustrate this cash versus forward difference, assume that both trades settle immediately; that is, the trade date is the same as the settlement date. Assume further that, to compare outlay only, the original principal amount for the forward trade is also $1 million. The total outlay of the cash trade is $1,001,325.71. It is derived from the market price of the principal at $1,003,125 plus an interim 29-day financing cost of $4,242.38 ($1,003,125 × 0.0525 × 29/360) minus a 29-day coupon income of $6,041.67 ($1,000,000 × 0.075 × 29/360). In an unchanged market, this outlay for the cash trade should be equal to that of the forward trade. Thus, the outlay of the forward trade will be $1,001,325.71. At $1 million principal, this implies a forward price of just above $100\frac{4}{32}$. This price reflects a drop of about 6 ticks, which is the break-even drop presented in Exhibit 2. When the actual forward market price is lower than $100\frac{4}{32}$, as in the hypothetical example of Exhibit 1, it reflects a market premium on the cash price influenced by the supply/demand factors.

Through time, as the forward trade date gradually approaches the cash trade date, the forward price accretes closer to the cash price. This occurs because the total outlay for the cash trade becomes more expensive as the coupon income (at 7.5%) shrinks faster than the reduction of financing cost (at 5.25%). For example, on 11/25/96, while there will be only 19 days of financing left, there also will be 19 days of coupon income. The total outlay for the cash trade therefore will grow to $1,001,946.16 ($1,003,125 + $2,779.49 − $3,958.33). To equate this total outlay, the forward price will elevate to around 100 6/32. The forward price will accrete further to just under 100 10/32 on 12/17/96 with only 1-day financing and 1-day coupon income. And it finally accretes to $100\frac{10}{32}$ on 12/18/96, when both financing and coupon income drop to zero, and the total outlay for the forward trade increases to $1,003,125. At this outlay, the forward price has accreted precisely to $100\frac{10}{32}$.

Chapter 10

Relative Value Analysis of Mortgage Securities

- Objective of Relative Value Analysis
- Bond Equivalent Yield Spread
- Holding Period Return
- Horizon Return
- Breakeven Prepayment Rate
- Analyzing Relative Value of REMICs

OBJECTIVE OF RELATIVE VALUE ANALYSIS

For mortgage securities, the objective of relative value analysis is to identify whether the value of a given coupon, under certain specifications in terms of WAC and WAM, is either rich or cheap relative to other coupons of mortgage securities. The analysis, often colloquially referred to as "rich/cheap" analysis, also assesses the value of mortgage securities versus their comparable average life Treasuries.

The relative value analysis of mortgage securities differs critically from that of corporate bonds in focus and scope. The focal point of the value of a mortgage security is the future prepayment behavior of its underlying mortgagors, whereas that of a corporate bond is the future credit quality of its issuer. The scope of the relative value analysis of mortgage securities is much more confined than that of corporate bonds. For practical purposes, the universe of mortgage securities is limited to a narrow range of coupons in a limited number of sectors. By contrast, the variety of corporate bonds is virtually unlimited. It proliferates constantly through the flotation of bonds by existing issuers as well as newly established corporate entities.

The universe of $1.7 trillion of outstanding mortgage securities belongs to only four sectors. They are distinguished by the guarantor of mortgage securities: Ginnie Mae, Fannie Mae, Freddie Mac, and private entities. The first three actually account for nearly 90% of the total. For all practical purposes, the coupon rate of securities within each sector ranges narrowly between 6% and 10%. The underlying pools of all these coupons consist of primarily 15- and 30-year fixed-rate mortgages, with a modest amount of 20-year fixed-rate mortgages, 5- and 7-year balloons, and adjustable-rate mortgages. The potential performance of all these coupons is essentially a function of future prepayments of their respective underlying mortgages under changing interest rates. While there are coupons outside the 6%-10% range, their outstanding balances are too small to warrant any active trading. In addition to market changes, their prices are very much influenced by "liquidity" — the amount of securities in supply and demand at any point in time.

Given the uniqueness of mortgage securities, several techniques have been developed to analyze their relative value. This chapter discusses four popular techniques: bond equivalent yield spread, holding period return, horizon return, and breakeven prepayment rate.

BOND EQUIVALENT YIELD SPREAD

One simplistic way of analyzing the relative value of a mortgage pass-through is to compare its current bond equivalent yield spread (hereafter, the yield spread) with its historical levels. As discussed in Chapter 5, the yield spread of a mortgage security is the difference between its bond equivalent yield and the yield of its comparable average life Treasury. A mortgage security of a specific coupon is considered cheap if its current yield spread is wider than its historical average, which conventionally covers a period of the past 12 months. Conversely, the security is rich if the current yield spread is tighter than the 12-month average.

For example, on June 17, 1996, new production 30-year GNMA 8.5s traded at $102^{13}/_{32}$. At 300% PSA, they had an expected average life of 5.5 years and yielded 7.95%. This yield was 122 basis points over the interpolated 5.5-year Treasury yield. (The yield on the interpolated 5.5-year Treasury is derived from the yields of on-the-run 5- and 10-year Treasuries.) Over the previous 12 months, this yield spread ranged mostly between 120 and 180 basis points, averaging 150. The yield spread analysis therefore suggests that GNMA 8.5s were rich because their current yield spread was not only tighter than the 12-month average but close to the tightest level of that period.

The yield spread analysis, however, is simplistic and has only a limited application. Moreover, it is useful only in a stable interest rate environment. The yield of a mortgage security is calculated under the assumption of a constant prepayment rate. This assumption is realistic only if interest rates remain stable. The sharp swing in interest rates in recent years has greatly limited the effectiveness of this analysis. This is particularly true in times of sharply declining interest rates, such as in 1995, when most coupons appreciated substantially. Their prepayments also accelerated to abnormally high levels. In this environment, market expectations of prepayments varied substantially, and a wide range of prepayment assumptions was used to compute yields of high premium coupons.

In late 1995, when interest rates were at a cyclical low, GNMA 8.5s appreciated to 105. At that price, the yield was 7.13% under 380% PSA with a yield spread of 177 basis points over the 4.6-year Treasury. But, if the prepayment assumption was accelerated to 480% PSA, as some market participants believed, the yield would be much lower at 6.77%. The yield spread would also be significantly tighter at 147 basis points over the 3.5-year Treasury. Based on the yield spread analysis, GNMA 8.5s would be cheap under the assumption of 380% PSA. However, under the assumption of 480% PSA, GNMA 8.5s would be rich. Thus, additional investigation was needed to judge the relative value of GNMA 8.5s. One additional analysis is to compute the security's holding period return.

HOLDING PERIOD RETURN

A mortgage security would be cheap if its current yield spread is wide by historical standards and has a greater total return over a holding period (holding period return) than other coupons and its comparable Treasury. The holding period return of a Treasury security or a corporate bond consists of three components: price appreciation (or depreciation), coupon return, and reinvestment of the coupon payment during the holding period. For mortgage securities, there is an additional and critical component — paydown of principal, both amortized repayment and prepayment. Thus, for mortgage securities, the component of reinvestment return includes interest earned on both the coupon and the principal. More important, because mortgages are prepaid at par, the paydown of principal enhances the return on coupons purchased at discount prices, but hinders the return of those acquired at premium prices.

In an environment of declining interest rates, prepayments of all coupons of mortgage securities rise rapidly. Premium coupons (premiums) will experience the sharpest increases in prepayments relative to discount and current coupons (discounts and currents). In this environment, discounts will far outperform premiums (even though premiums have a higher coupon income) for basically two reasons: greater price appreciation and a significant benefit from principal returned at par. In fact, these two factors reinforce each other. Falling interest rates raise the price of discounts. Meanwhile, they also heighten prepayments, which further enhance total returns. By contrast, declining interest rates impair the performance of premium coupons by accelerating principal paydown at par, which in turn limits price appreciation. This limitation is termed *price compression* of premium coupons.

From the holding period return analysis, 30-year GNMA 6s in the beginning of 1996 were cheap relative to 30-year GNMA 9s. Exhibit 1 shows that the annual 1995 return of GNMA 6s was a stunning 23.1%, dwarfing the 11.3% return produced by GNMA 9.5s. GNMA 6s outperformed GNMA 9.5s on two fronts: price appreciation and prepayment acceleration. In fact, in 1995, the lower the coupon, the greater was its performance. As is detailed in Exhibit 2, while the price appreciation of GNMA 6s was the decisive factor in their superior return, the 0.81% return due to principal paydown also contributed to their stellar performance. By contrast, not only did GNMA 9.5s have a mediocre price performance, they also suffered a negative return of 0.59% due to the accelerated par paydown of principal, which was acquired at the beginning of 1995 at a price of 103¹/₃₂.

Exhibit 1: Holding Period Returns of Selected 30-Year GNMAs, January 1 to December 31, 1995
(Based on an Original Principal of $1,000)

	GNMA 6s	GNMA 7s	GNMA 7.5s	GNMA 8s	GNMA 8.5s	GNMA 9s	GNMA 9.5s
Beginning Price (32nds)	83-5	89-18	92-19	95-14	98-3	100-25	103-1
Initial Investment ($)	831.56	895.63	925.94	954.38	980.94	1,007.81	1,030.31
Prepayment ($)	39.94	68.00	91.10	114.30	182.29	193.02	201.02
Coupon Income ($)	54.00	62.16	65.86	69.44	71.23	74.98	85.13
Reinvestment Income ($)	1.96	2.74	3.31	3.90	5.45	5.77	6.04
Ending Price (32nds)	97-9	101-6	102-28	104-7	105-1	105-31	107-11
Total Proceeds ($)	1,034.66	1,081.40	1,100.98	1,116.61	1,123.61	1,134.97	1,149.84
Holding Period Return (%)	24.42	20.74	18.91	17.00	14.54	12.62	11.60
Bond Eqi. Return (%)	23.09	19.77	18.09	16.33	14.05	12.24	11.28

Source: Oppenheimer & Co., Inc. and BLOOMBERG Financial Markets

Exhibit 2: Components of Holding Period Returns of GNMA 6s and 9.5s, January 1 to December 31, 1995

	GNMA 6s (%)	GNMA 9.5s (%)
Impact of Prepayments	0.81	−0.59
Coupon Income	7.07	8.26
Reinvestment Income	0.24	0.59
Price Appreciation	16.31	3.34
Holding Period Return	24.42	11.60

Source: Oppenheimer & Co., Inc. and BLOOMBERG Financial Markets

HORIZON RETURN

As demonstrated above, the holding period return analysis evaluates mortgage securities more completely than the yield spread analysis because it takes into consideration their performance in the recent past. However, holding period returns still tell only half of the story by evaluating mortgage securities in a historical context. To complete the relative value story, the total return concept should be applied to a future period. A horizon return analysis should be conducted.

For example, a discount coupon maybe deemed cheap not only because of its wide yield spread and great holding period return, but its potentially strong performance in the future under various interest rate scenarios. On the other hand, the discount coupon may eventually be considered rich, despite its wide spread and great historical performance, if its probability-weighted horizon return under various interest rates is low relative to other coupons or the comparable Treasury.

A horizon analysis assesses the prospective performance of a mortgage security over a given holding period in the future under various interest rate scenarios. For each interest rate scenario, the analysis makes four important assumptions:

Exhibit 3: Probability-Weighted One-Year Horizon Returns of Selected 30-Year New Production GNMAs, as of June 28, 1996

Interest Rate Scenario	Probability	Return (%) for								
		6s	7s	7.5s	8s	8.5s	9.5s	3-Yr Tsy	5-Yr Tsy	10-Yr Tsy
decline 150 bps	1.8	15.98	13.97	12.58	11.02	9.80	7.80	8.41	11.24	16.53
decline 100 bps	10.1	13.20	12.63	12.16	10.08	9.19	7.26	7.62	9.57	13.10
decline 50 bps	24.6	10.41	10.23	10.03	8.90	8.45	6.92	6.83	7.92	9.75
Unchanged	30.0	7.28	7.49	7.54	7.65	7.44	6.78	6.05	6.30	6.48
rise 50 bps	20.8	4.16	4.78	4.80	5.50	5.98	5.82	5.28	4.69	3.30
rise 100 bps	9.1	0.90	1.76	1.98	2.81	4.44	5.36	4.51	3.11	0.21
rise 150 bps	3.5	−2.20	−1.14	−0.85	0.01	1.91	4.50	3.74	1.54	−2.81
Prob.-Weighted Total Return (%)	100	7.24	7.41	7.33	7.11	7.15	6.48	6.06	6.32	6.58

Source: Oppenheimer & Co., Inc. and BLOOMBERG Financial Markets

- prepayment rates during and after the horizon period
- the yield spread at the end of the horizon period (Along with projected prepayment rates, this assumption provides the selling price of the mortgage security.)
- the reinvestment rate during the holding period for the principal paydown and coupon payment
- probability weights of the interest rate scenarios.

The numerical example provided in Exhibit 3 demonstrates the potential performance of selected GNMAs over the next 12 months. During this period, interest rates are assumed either to remain unchanged, or to rise/decline 50, 100, or 150 basis points, respectively. Under each of these scenarios, mortgage yields are assumed to move parallel to the Treasury yield curve. Appropriate prepayments under each interest rate scenario are projected for the selected GNMA coupons. The analysis further assumes consistent short-term rates for the reinvestment of the principal paydown and the coupon return.

As shown in Exhibit 3, over a 12-month horizon, if interest rates remain unchanged, all GNMAs would outperform their respective comparable Treasuries. (For convenience, in this analysis, the comparable Treasury for GNMA 6s to 8s is the 10-year Treasury; for GNMA 8.5s, the 5-year Treasury; for GNMA 9s and 9.5s, the 3-year Treasury.) The winning factor of GNMAs is that their yields markedly exceed those of Treasuries. In terms of the components of the total return, the excess yields are mainly in coupon income. With unchanged interest rates, there would be little change in the selling prices of all coupons. GNMAs with a greater coupon income would naturally outperform all Treasuries.

If interest rates decline 50 basis points, all discount coupon GNMA 6s to 7.5s would still comfortably outstrip comparable Treasuries in total returns. Treasuries are known to have a greater price appreciation than mortgage securities in a bond market rally. However, their greater margin of price performance is more than offset by the larger coupon income of GNMAs. Nevertheless, if interest rates decline more than 100 basis points, all GNMAs (except the 6s) would fall behind comparable Treasuries. In these scenarios, Treasuries win on two accounts. First, the price appreciation of Treasuries now outweighs the coupon income of most GNMAs. Second, expected acceleration in prepayments hinders the performance of most coupons.

The stellar performance of GNMA 6s up to a 100 basis point decline in interest rates is due to their ability to maintain a long average life. This feature enables GNMA 6s to keep pace with the 10-year Treasury in a strong market rally. Also, because of their deeply discounted prices, GNMA 6s benefit rather than suffer when prepayments accelerate. However, if interest rates drop 150 basis points, even GNMA 6s would be outrun by the comparable Treasury. By contrast, the significantly lower horizon return of high-premium GNMA 9.5s relative to the 3-year Treasury in a market rally is caused by the lack of price appreciation due to expected acceleration of prepayments.

Conversely, all GNMAs would consistently outperform comparable Treasuries if interest rates rise 50, 100, or 150 basis points. This reflects the bearish nature of mortgage pass-throughs. Although their prices decline in a bearish market like all fixed income securities, the magnitude of the decline is mitigated by the cushion of their coupons. Because of this cushion, mortgage securities are able to produce either greater positive or smaller negative returns than comparable Treasuries. For premium coupons, total returns of mortgage securities decline only grudgingly as interest rates rise. And the higher the coupon, the smaller is the decline in total returns. The resilience of premium coupons in a bearish market is attributable to the *price decompression*, which contrasts with their behavior in a market rally.

On a probability-weighted basis, the horizon total returns of mortgage securities in the seven interest rate scenarios reveal that mortgage securities are generally cheap to Treasuries. Among mortgage securities themselves, discounts are cheap to premiums. In particular, GNMA 7s have the greatest horizon return. This, coupled with their currently wide yield spread and strong performance in 1995, suggests that GNMA 7s are cheap. By contrast, GNMA 9.5s are rich. Not only is their current yield spread historically tight and 1995 return weak, but their horizon return is the lowest among all coupons.

Conceptually, the horizon return analysis can be simplified by assuming a "constant OAS." As briefly mentioned in Chapter 5, one important application of option-adjusted spread is for the computation of horizon returns. By assuming that the OAS of a mortgage security remains unchanged, the horizon analysis no longer needs to make assumptions of prepayments, end-period yield spreads, and selling prices for mortgage securities. These assumptions are arbitrary and could be biased. The "constant OAS" horizon returns provide a more objective assessment of the relative value of mortgage securities by requiring all securities to maintain a constant yield spread after netting out the option cost under various interest rate environments. A mortgage security of a given coupon is then considered cheap if it can still provide a greater probability-weighted return than other coupons.

BREAKEVEN PREPAYMENT RATE

Given the price of a mortgage security (30- or 15-year), there is a corresponding breakeven prepayment rate such that the security's yield spread is identical to that of its benchmark (current) coupon. At the breakeven rate, investors would be indifferent towards purchasing any coupon since they all provide the same yield spread over their respective comparable Treasuries. This is a simple but useful concept. It helps market participants formulate a long-term perspective of prepayments for various coupons of mortgage securities. In the current market, where mortgage rates have been volatile with prepayment expectations varying substantially, the concept of a breakeven prepayment rate is particularly helpful.

The benchmark-coupon yield spread for a 30-year mortgage passthrough can be defined as the weighted average yield spread of the highest discount and lowest premium coupon 30-year GNMAs. For example, in June 1996, the two coupons are 30-year GNMA 7.5s and 8s. The weight is determined by the price difference between the coupon and par. It is important to note that the closer the coupon's price is to par, the greater is its weight. On June 14, GNMA 7.5s and 8s traded at $97^{18}/_{32}$ and $100^{4}/_{32}$ to yield 7.99% and 8.05% with yield spreads of 105 and 114 basis points, respectively. The sum of the differences of the two coupons to the par price is $^{8}2/_{32}$ ($100 - 97^{18}/_{32}$, or $2^{14}/_{32}$ of the 7.5s, and $100^{4}/_{32} - 100$, or $^{4}/_{32}$ of the 8s). The weight for GNMA 8s, whose price is closer to par, is therefore $^{78}/_{82}$, or 95.1%; for GNMA 7.5s, $^{4}/_{82}$, or 4.9%. The benchmark coupon yield spread therefore is 109 ($0.951 \times 114 + 0.049 \times 105$). Since the breakeven definition involves two coupons whose prices are closest to par, these two coupons do not have a breakeven prepayment rate.

The breakeven rate basically reflects the implied market expectations of prepayments of various coupons. Individual investors, however, may or may not agree with these expectations. In that sense, the breakeven rate has implications for inter-coupon relative values. Investors may decide to purchase a premium coupon if its breakeven rate is significantly high by their judgment. This judgment may be formed through observations of historical prepayments along with current economic, housing, and demographic factors. If future prepayments do drop below the breakeven rate, the price of the premium coupon will appreciate (assuming more or less unchanged interest rates). Conversely, investors may want to sell a discount coupon based on the belief that its breakeven rate is too high. If prepayments in fact turn lower in the future, the discount coupon will depreciate.

Exhibit 4 provides breakeven prepayment rates for selected 30-year GNMAs. For example, the breakeven prepayment rate for GNMA 6s is 125% PSA. It means that long-term prepayments have to rise to 125% PSA, an increase of 25% PSA from the pricing speed, for GNMA 6s to provide the same yield spread over the 10.5-year Treasury as the benchmark coupon.

The breakeven analysis reveals that new production discounts (6s to 7s) are slightly rich to the benchmark coupon because their prepayments have to rise to a range of 125% and 161% PSA to provide the same yield spread as the benchmark coupon. This range is moderately higher than the housing turnover rate, which is the predominant factor of their prepayments. As defined in Chapter 4, the housing turnover rate is a ratio of annual sales of existing homes to the stock of occupied single-family houses. Currently, the turnover rate is 6%, or 100% PSA.

The breakeven analysis indicates different relative values for premiums (8.5s to 9.5s). GNMA 9.5s are rich because their prepayments have to decline almost 100% PSA from the pricing speed in order to match the benchmark coupon's yield spread. By contrast, GNMA 8.5s are cheap. Their future prepayments can accelerate almost 100% PSA from the current pricing speed and still be as attractive as the benchmark coupon. GNMA 9s, however, are fairly priced, as their breakeven prepayment rate is about the same as the pricing speed.

One reason that most coupons inevitably seem rich according to the breakeven analysis is that the benchmark coupon yield spread itself is cheap. Indeed, its yield spread of 109 basis points is close to the cheapest level since mid-1990. At this level, no other coupons can easily be more attractive than the benchmark coupon. This is particularly true for discounts. Traditionally, discounts have tighter yield spreads than the benchmark coupon. Nevertheless, the breakeven concept is still useful in that it measures how fast discounts have to prepay in order to provide equally attractive yield spreads. If the required acceleration is moderate, as in the present case, discounts may still be relatively attractive.

The breakeven analysis is more useful to detect relative value among premiums. Their yield spreads are usually wider than the benchmark coupon. As such, if their speeds have to decelerate significantly in order to compete with the benchmark coupon, then it is clear that these coupons are rich.

Exhibit 4: Breakeven Prepayment Rates for Selected New Production 30-Year GNMAs, As of June 14, 1996

Coupon (%)	Price (1/32)	Yield (%)	Yld Sprd (bp, Tsy)	Pricing PSA (%)	Breakeven PSA (%)	Breakeven Minus Pricing PSA (%)
6	88-27	7.88	93, 10.5	100	125	25
6.5	91-26	7.94	100, 10.1	115	135	20
7	94-25	7.93	99, 10.3	120	161	41
7.5	97-18	7.99	105, 9.8	130	N. A.	N. A.
8	100-04	8.05	114, 8.3	180	N. A.	N. A.
8.5	102-13	7.95	118, 5.5	300	398	98
9	104-13	7.70	105, 4.4	350	341	-9
9.5	106-27	7.15	59, 3.7	400	301	-99

Source: Oppenheimer & Co., Inc.

ANALYZING RELATIVE VALUE OF REMICS

Since REMICs are derived from mortgage pass-throughs, the analysis of their relative values relies on the same techniques as described above. However, because the cash flow of a REMIC bond class (hereafter, bond class) is uniquely segmented from the underlying pass-through collateral, more attention has to be given to the specific structure of the cash flow. This is particularly so in view of the size and diversity of the REMIC market. Currently, there are nearly 2,000 REMICs outstanding with many thousands of bond classes and a total outstanding principal balance of more than $750 billion. It is safe to say that no two bond classes are structured exactly the same with identical cash flows. However, for relative value analysis, the marketplace creates a "generic" bond class. It is defined as a bond class backed by new production 30-year current coupon collateral. For example, while no two PACs are structurally the same, there is a generic PAC whose yield spread serves as a benchmark for the comparison of the relative value for hundreds of PACs that are outstanding.

The following example illustrates the various features of a randomly selected bond class that need to be analyzed to determine its relative value.

Consider FHR 1856 VB (Class VB), a 7% coupon accretion directed sequential backed by FHLMC Gold 30-year 8s with a WAM of 352 months. On July 23, 1996, it was priced at 100^{16}/32 and 135% PSA to yield 7.48% with an expected average life of 7.57 years (Exhibit 5). This yield was 70 basis points over the interpolated 7.6-year Treasury. Features of its cash flow that have an important impact on its relative value are as follows:

Exhibit 5: Price/Yield Analysis and Cash Flow Characteristics of FHR 1856 Class VB

G35 **Mtge**   **Y T**

Note: Projections start with 7/15/1996 payment.

Bloomberg   F H R   1 8 5 6   V B   7.5% 6/15/ 6   ADV:<PAGE>
CMO I I   3133T7B32   CMO:ACCRETION DIRECTED   [No Band   6/96] NO Notes 88 <Go>

FGLMC 8 N   8.514(352)6 WAC(WAM)WALA JUL96

| JUL 1mo 1112P 12.9¢
'96 3mo - -
6mo - -
12mo - -
Life 1112 12.9 | 6/28/96: 12,814,600
7/15/96: 12,814,600
factor 1.000000000000 | next pay 8/15/96 (monthly)
rcd date 7/31/96 (14 Delay)
accrual 7/ 1/96- 7/31/96 | 30/360 Cashflows
created 6/13/96
1stProj 7/15/96
ASSUMED collateral |

7/26/96   Y I E L D   T A B L E

| Vary
PRICE 1 32 | 135
135 PSA | 0
0 PSA | 250
250 PSA | 300
300 PSA | 350
350 PSA | 500
500 PSA | 700
700 PSA |

DEAL: Freddie Mac Modifiable and Combinable REMIC ("MACR")
CUR GEO DIST (07/96): CA 17.1% FL 9.6% MI 8.6% NY 7.7% IL 5.6% OTHER 51.4%

| 100-16 | 7.476 | 7.476 | 7.476 | 7.474 | 7.468 | 7.439 | 7.387 |

AvgLife	7.57	7.57	7.57	7.41	7.00	5.55	4.11
Mod Dur	5.54	5.54	5.54	5.47	5.25	4.39	3.41
DATEWindow	6/01- 6/15/06	6/01- 6/15/06	6/01- 6/15/06	6/01- 6/15/05	6/01- 6/15/04	6/01- 6/15/02	6/00- 11/15/00
Tsy Sprd I	+75/AL	+75/AL	+75/AL	+75/AL	+77/AL	+80/AL	+86/AL

NEVER CALLED   Preliminary cashflows based upon dealer representations. PROSPECTUS UNAVAILABLE.

Treasury Curve - BGN 14:04
3mo 6mo -1- -2- -3- -5- -10- -30-
5.30 5.54 5.87 6.24 6.41 6.62 6.83 7.00

Format# 1-YT 1%Cleanup

Source: BLOOMBERG Financial Markets

Stability of average life. First and foremost, despite being a sequential class, the average life of Class VB is remarkably stable when prepayments vary between 0% and 300% PSA. Within this prepayment range, the average life of Class VB varies by less than 0.2 year. Additionally, even at a 350% PSA, the average life shortens only slightly to 7 years. At an exceedingly fast speed of 700% PSA, the average life shortens by a little over 3 years to 4.1 years. Historically, prepayments of new production FHLMC Gold 8s exceeded 700% PSA only briefly in late 1993 and early 1994, when mortgage rates first dropped below 7.5%. As soon as mortgage rates rose above 8% in mid-1994, prepayments plunged to below 200% PSA. In order for FHLMC Gold 8s to prepay at 300% to 400% PSA on a long-term basis, mortgage rates would have to stay constant at around 7%. This rate is 150 basis points below the current level. If future mortgage rates remain around 8.5% or higher, FHLMC Gold 8s are likely to prepay either at or moderately below the pricing speed of 135% PSA. In this case, the average life of Class VB is rock stable at 7.57 years.

Stability of final maturity. At a theoretically worst case of a 0% PSA, Class VB is a 10-year bond with a final maturity date of June 15, 2006. Conversely, at an extremely fast speed of 700% PSA, the maturity of Class VB shortens to 4.1 years with a final maturity date of November 15, 2000. However, in a more realistic range of prepayment speeds, between 135% and 350% PSA, the final maturity is quite stable. It varies between 8 and 10 years.

Prepayment lockout period. At the pricing of 135% PSA, the first payment of principal will not take place until June 2001. In fact, this is true between 0% and 250% PSA. Even under an extreme 700% PSA, the first principal payment date accelerates only one year to June 2000. Thus, Class VB has a virtually minimum principal prepayment lockout of four years.

Tightness of prepayment window. In addition to a long lockout period, the window period of Class VB (first to last payment dates of principal) is tight. Under the pricing speed, it has a five-year window period, June 2001 to June 2006. At 350% PSA, the window period shortens by only two years: from June 2001 to June 2004. Although the window period shortens to just five months under a 700% PSA, the first principal prepayment, as mentioned above, does not take place until June 2000.

Comparison of yield spreads. Class VB yields 75 basis points over the 7.57-year Treasury. Between 0% and 350% PSA, the average life of Class VB varies between 7.7 and 7.1 years. With this stable average life, its yield spread is 10 basis points wider than generic comparable average life

PACs backed by new production 30-year 7s. Class VB's yield spread, however, is about 20 basis points tighter than generic sequentials backed by 30-year 7s. But the average life of a generic sequential is significantly more volatile than Class VB with a much wider window. Also, the yield spread of Class VB is about 5 to 10 basis point tighter than that of new production FNMA/FHLMC 15-year 7s, which have an expected average life slightly shorter than 7 years. But, Class VB has a much shorter final maturity with a prepayment lockout period — the two features that are far superior to new production FNMA/FHLMC 15-year 7s.

The investigation of the above features points out the risk/reward analysis that is important for REMIC classes. Because REMIC classes are structured differently, there are inevitable trade-offs among the many features of bond classes. And these trade-offs determine the relative value. Class VB may be cheap relative to comparable average life PACs for yield oriented investors who overlook the aspect of absolute stability of average life within a range of prepayments. However, for investors who can tolerate a greater variation of average life or final maturity, Class VB may be rich to comparable average life sequentials. For investors who have even more tolerance of average life fluctuation, the comparable average life single-class pass-throughs that provide still greater yield spreads may be cheap to Class VB.

To sum up, for any bond class, investors need to investigate at a minimum the following features to determine its relative value: coupon rate of the bond class, the WAM and the WAC of the underlying collateral, historical prepayments of the collateral, expected average lives and final maturities of the bond class at various prepayment scenarios, the prepayment lockout and window period, and yield spreads under various prepayments.

Chapter 11

Performance of
Mortgage Securities

- Determinants of the Benchmark Yield Spread
- Movement of the Benchmark Yield Spread and Total Return

Like the old saying, "the proof of the pudding is in the eating," the attractiveness of fixed-income securities is in the performance. The performance of mortgage-backed securities is reflected by their annual total return. According to the Merrill Lynch Global Index System, over a 10.5-year period between January 1986 and June 1996, mortgage securities produced an annualized return of 9.11%. This performance bested Treasuries of all maturities by 40 basis points annually.

While on a long-term basis mortgage securities have proved to be superior to Treasuries, it is not necessarily so on a short-term basis for a calendar year or a given holding period. In terms of calendar year performance, mortgage securities outperformed Treasuries in seven of the past 10 years (Exhibit 1). With respect to certain holding periods, however, mortgage securities have demonstrated mixed performance versus Treasuries. Particularly, in recent years, mortgage securities have underperformed Treasuries. This has been the result of significant fluctuation of interest rates and, more important, the widening of mortgage yield spreads.

Exhibit 1: Total Annual Returns of Mortgage Securities and Treasuries, 1986 to 1995

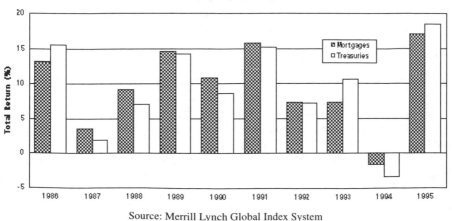

Source: Merrill Lynch Global Index System

In this final chapter, the performance of mortgage securities versus those of Treasuries in several sub-periods of widening or tightening mortgage yield spreads between January 1986 and June 1996 is reviewed. As part of the review, this chapter also explains the factors that influence mortgage yield spreads, and how they affect the performance of mortgage-backed securities.

DETERMINANTS OF THE BENCHMARK YIELD SPREAD

As a convention, mortgage yield spreads are represented by the difference between benchmark-coupon yield of 30-year GNMAs and the 10-year Treasury yield. As explained in Chapter 10, the benchmark-coupon yield is defined as the weighted average yield of the highest discount- and the lowest premium-coupon GNMAs. Between January 1986 and June 1996, the monthly benchmark-coupon yield spread (hereafter, the benchmark yield spread) fluctuated between 66 and 222 basis points. In the early 1990s, the benchmark yield spread tightened dramatically. By mid-1992, it tightened to the low end of this range. Since then, it has widened. In particular, between mid-1995 and mid-1996, the benchmark yield spread has widened significantly back to a range of 110 to 120 basis points.

Between January 1986 and June 1996, many factors have influenced the level of the benchmark yield spread. (The study period begins with 1986 because it was the first year of REMICs, which have had a profound impact on the performance of mortgage securities.) They include: the level of interest rates, the shape of the Treasury yield curve, issuance of REMICs and mortgage pass-throughs, bond market volatility, housing activity, and the origination market share of FRMs versus ARMs. Other things being constant, the individual relationships between these factors and the benchmark yield spread follow.

Level of the 10-Year Treasury Yield

The level of the 10-year Treasury yield has a positive influence on the benchmark yield spread. The benchmark coupon yield is the weighted average yield of the highest new-production discount and the lowest new-production premium coupons. However, the theoretical price of the benchmark coupon is always around par, regardless of the level of the 10-year Treasury yield. At par, the benchmark-coupon yield moves in the same direction as the 10-year Treasury yield. Additionally, new production 30-year pass-throughs have longer expected average lives than most coupons and are usually priced off the 10-year Treasury. In a market rally, investors tend to "move down" in coupon to maintain the average life of their mortgage portfolios. In a market retreat, they "move up" in coupon to prevent average life extension. Thus, on a relative basis, the benchmark yield spread tends to move in the same direction as the yield of the 10-year Treasury (see Exhibit 2).

Exhibit 2: The Benchmark Mortgage Yield Spread and the 10-Year Treasury Yield, 1/86 to 6/96

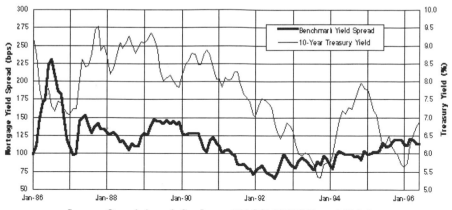

Sources: Oppenheimer & Co., Inc. and BLOOMBERG Financial Markets

Exhibit 3: The Benchmark Mortgage Yield Spread and the 10-Year/2-Year Treasury Yield Spread, 1/86 to 6/96

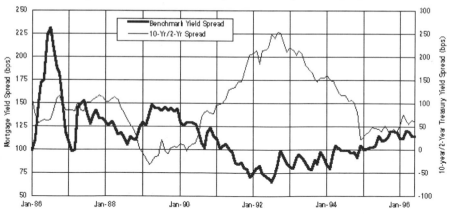

Sources: Oppenheimer & Co., Inc. and BLOOMBERG Financial Markets

Shape of the Treasury Yield Curve

The shape of the Treasury yield curve — measured by the yield difference between the 10- and 2-year Treasuries — has been inversely associated with the benchmark yield spread. As the curve steepens (the 10- to 2-year yield spread widens), the benchmark yield spread tightens, and vice versa (see Exhibit 3). This relationship has been particularly significant since the late-1980s, as REMICs played an increasingly important role in the pricing of mortgage securities. Through the multiple maturity classes of REMICs, the underlying collateral of mortgage pass-throughs is priced along the Treasury yield curve. (Prior to

REMICs, the pricing had been essentially off just one spot of the curve — the 10-year Treasury.) This "REMIC arbitrage" enables mortgage pass-throughs to take advantage of the positive slope of the Treasury curve and achieve higher price levels. In other words, it improves the efficiency of pricing mortgage pass-throughs. This is the most important reason why the level of the benchmark yield spread had become markedly tighter in the late 1980s and the early 1990s.

Issuance of REMICs and Mortgage Pass-Throughs

From the yield curve discussion, it stands to reason that an increase in the issuance of REMICs tightens the benchmark yield spread (see Exhibit 4). Additionally, because REMICs are created primarily out of newly issued mortgage pass-throughs, an increase in REMIC issuance raises the demand for pass-throughs. Given the supply, an increase in the demand for newly issued pass-throughs for REMIC purposes actually reduces the availability of newly issued pass-throughs. This reduction tightens the benchmark yield spread. Thus, by netting REMICs out of newly issued pass-throughs, the net issuance of pass-throughs tends to be positively related to the benchmark yield spread (see Exhibit 5).

Bond Market Volatility

Volatility here is defined as the annualized 20-day standard deviation of the daily percent change in the 10-year Treasury yield. It is positively associated with the benchmark yield spread. In essence, the mortgage yield spread is compensation to investors in mortgage securities for providing the prepayment option to homeowners. The premium of that option is positively dependent on volatility: the greater the volatility, the more valuable is the option. Therefore, in a volatile interest rate environment, investors in mortgage securities need to be compensated more by a wider yield spread. (See Exhibit 6.)

Exhibit 4: The Benchmark Mortgage Yield Spread and Monthly REMIC Issuance, 1/86 to 6/96

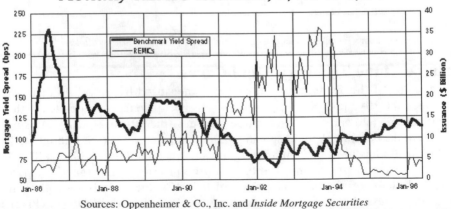

Sources: Oppenheimer & Co., Inc. and *Inside Mortgage Securities*

Exhibit 5: The Benchmark Mortgage Yield Spread and Net Issuance of Pass-Throughs, 1/86 to 6/96

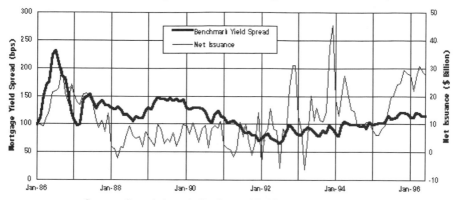

Sources: Oppenheimer & Co., Inc. and Inside Mortgage Securities
Reprinted with permission of Inside Mortgage Securities, Copyright 1996, Bethesda, Maryland. (301-951-1240)

Exhibit 6: The Benchmark Mortgage Yield Spread and the Volatility of the 10-Year Treasury Yield, 1/86 to 6/96

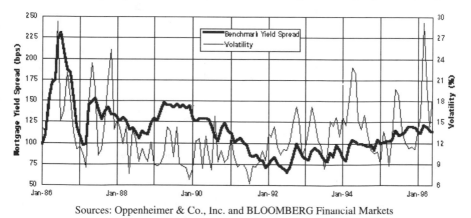

Sources: Oppenheimer & Co., Inc. and BLOOMBERG Financial Markets

Housing Activity

The benchmark yield spread is a positive function of housing activity, measured here by monthly single-family housing starts. The fundamental purpose of mortgages is to finance the demand for housing. In a way, the mortgage yield spread represents the interest rate premium that homeowners have to pay for housing finance. Strong housing activity heightens the demand for mortgage credit and raises the premium of mortgage credit. It therefore widens the benchmark yield spread (see Exhibit 7).

Exhibit 7: The Benchmark Mortgage Yield Spread and SIngle Family Housing Starts, 1/86 to 6/96

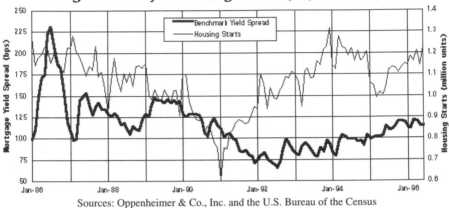

Sources: Oppenheimer & Co., Inc. and the U.S. Bureau of the Census

Exhibit 8: The Benchmark Mortgage Yield Spread and Origination Market Share of FRMs, 1/86 to 6/96

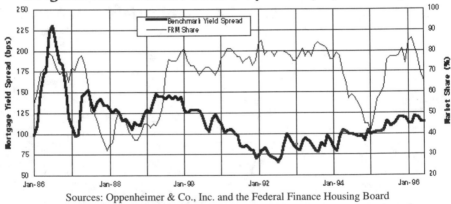

Sources: Oppenheimer & Co., Inc. and the Federal Finance Housing Board

Origination Market Share of FRMs

Prior to the late-1980s before the full development of REMICs, the origination market share of FRMs had been positively related to the benchmark yield spread: a rising market share of FRMs widened the benchmark yield spread (see Exhibit 8). The demand for mortgage credit can be satisfied through originations of either FRMs or ARMs. In general, FRMs are funded in the form of pass-throughs in the capital markets. They have a larger investor base. By contrast, ARMs are funded mostly by thrifts and banks through deposits. In an environment of low interest rates with home buyers mostly opting for FRM financing, the strong pressure to fund FRMs tends to widen the benchmark yield spread. Conversely, in high interest rates, home buyers seek ARM financing as a cheaper alternative. This alternative reduces the pressure to fund FRMs and reduces the yield spread.

MOVEMENT OF THE BENCHMARK YIELD SPREAD AND TOTAL RETURN

The 10.5 years between January 1986 and June 1996 can be subdivided into seven sub-periods, where the benchmark yield spread widened or tightened significantly. With only one minor exception, mortgage securities outperformed Treasuries of all maturities when the benchmark yield spread tightened, and underperformed Treasuries when the spread widened. The seven sub-periods, along with the movement of the benchmark yield spread and the performance of mortgage securities on a holding period return basis versus Treasuries of all maturities, are briefly discussed below and summarized in Exhibit 9.

Widening Yield Spread, January 1986 to July 1986
The benchmark yield spread widened in just six months from 99 to 231 basis points, and mortgage securities underperformed Treasuries in holding period return by 443 basis points (6.91% versus 11.34%). Generally speaking, mortgage securities are inherently bearish with negative convexity. Their prices appreciate less than comparable Treasuries in a significant rally. That was clearly the case in this period, when the powerful bond market rally pushed the 10-year Treasury yield down nearly 200 basis points in six months from a monthly average of 9.19% to 7.30%. This dramatic rally also heightened volatility from 14.2% to 29.3%, a level almost on par with the record highs that prevailed in the early 1980s. These events, coupled with strong housing activity and the expanding market share of FRMs, substantially widened the benchmark yield spread and caused the underperformance of mortgage securities.

Tightening Yield Spread, July 1986 to February 1987
The benchmark yield spread reversed itself completely in this period, tightening from 231 to 98 basis points. With a holding period return of 10.41%, mortgage securities outperformed Treasuries by 368 basis points. Mortgage securities were able to turn the tide due primarily to the sharp decline in volatility, as the decline in interest rates moderated. Further, with the beginning of the expansion of REMICs, the pricing of mortgage securities became more efficient. Moreover, the benchmark coupon rate also fell along with the drop in the 10-year Treasury yield.

Widening Yield Spread, February 1987 to June 1987
The benchmark yield spread made another about-face, widening from 98 to 153 basis points. In this short period, the 10-year Treasury surged 115 basis points from 7.25% to 8.4%. But mortgage securities weathered the storm of rising rates better than Treasuries with a smaller negative holding period return (−1.14% versus −1.68%). This exception may be explained by the shorter duration of mortgage securities. In a major market retreat, mortgage securities suffered a smaller price loss than Treasuries. This advantage outweighed the widening of the benchmark yield spread. Another explanation could be that mortgage securities lagged Treasuries so much during the rally in early 1986 that they were better able to resist the downward price pressure as the market retreated.

Exhibit 9: Holding Period Returns (HPRs) of Mortgage Securities and Treasuries in Periods of Major Widening or Tightening of the Benchmark Yield Spread, January 1986 to June 1996

Period	Change in the Benchmark Yield Spread (basis point)	Mtg HPR (%)	Treasury HPR (%)	HPR Mtg vs Tsy (basis point)	Characteristics of Period
1/86 to 7/86	Widening: 99 to 231	6.91	11.34	-443	1. Powerful bond market rally 2. Surging volatility 3. Strong demand for mortgage credit 4. Large market share of FRM originations
7/86 to 2/87	Tightening: 231 to 98	10.41	6.73	368	1. Plunging volatility 2. Initial expansion of REMICs 3. Sharp drop in benchmark coupon yield
2/87 to 6/87	Widening: 98 to 153	-1.14	-1.68	54	1. Surging volatility 2. Sharp rise in interest rates
6/87 to 8/88	Tightening: 153 to 105	11.41	7.67	374	1. Plunging volatility 2. Continued rise in fixed mortgage rates 3. Increasing popularity of ARMs
8/88 to 4/89	Widening: 105 to 148	6.13	6.53	-40	1. Inverted yield curve 2. Strong FRM originations 3. Liquidation of mortgage assets by thrifts
4/89 to 7/92	Tightening: 148 to 66	51.52	48.08	344	1. Record steep Treasury yield curve 2. Exceedingly strong REMICs 3. Weakened demand for mortgage credit
7/92 to 6/96	Widening: 66 to 114	28.41	30.46	-205	1. Persistently flat Treasury yield curve 2. Heightened volatility 3. REMICs collapsed from record strength 4. Predominant market share of FRMs 5. Stunning recovery of housing activity

Notes:

Shaded area represents exception to the normal relationship between the movement of the benchmark yield spread and mortgage securities' performance relative to Treasuries. Mortgage securities include all three sectors and all final maturities and Treasuries include all maturities.

Sources: Oppenheimer & Co., Inc. and Merrill Lynch Global Index System

Tightening Yield Spread, June 1987 to August 1988

The benchmark yield spread tightened from 153 to 105 basis points. Mortgages returned 11.41% for this period, 374 basis points more than Treasuries. Mortgage securities benefited from a steady but modest rise in interest rates and an environment of low volatility. Further, rising interest rates made ARMs increasingly popular among home buyers. This in turn reduced the pressure to fund FRMs and tightened the benchmark yield spread.

Widening Yield Spread, August 1988 to April 1989

The benchmark yield spread widened from 105 to 148 basis points. While the 6.13%% total return for a short 9-month period of mortgage securities was respectable, it was still 40 basis points behind that of Treasuries. The relatively smaller REMIC issuance, which was caused by the inverted Treasury yield curve, pressured the yield spread to widen. Also exerting a widening pressure was the expanding origination market share of FRMs. Additionally, during this period, thrift institutions went through a major balance-sheet restructuring by liquidating mortgage assets. The liquidation helped sustain a wider yield spread.

Tightening Yield Spread, April 1989 to July 1992

This was the brightest period for mortgage securities. The benchmark yield spread tightened from 148 to 66 basis points amid the first leg of one of the most powerful bond-market rallies in history. The 10-year Treasury yield dropped 234 basis points from 9.18% to 6.84%. Despite the rally, mortgage securities performed better than Treasuries (a holding period return of 51.52% versus 48.08%). This superior performance was due primarily to the dramatic tightening of the yield spread in the environment of a record steep Treasury yield curve. The steepness of the yield curve facilitated enormous issuance of REMICs, which reduced the net amount of newly issued mortgage pass-throughs. Further, despite the persistently large market share of FRM originations, depressed housing activity lowered the pressure to fund FRMs and maintained a tight yield spread.

Widening Yield Spread, July 1992 to June 1996

The benchmark yield spread oscillated and widened from 66 to 114 basis points and mortgage securities underperformed Treasuries by 205 basis points (28.41% versus 30.46%). This was one of the most eventful and difficult periods for mortgage securities. Interest rates fluctuated widely throughout the period and the Treasury yield curve remained historically flat for a significant part of this period. Between July 1992 and October 1993, the 10-year Treasury yield dropped 150 basis points to a historic low of 5.3%. However, it quickly escalated by 230 basis points to almost 8% during 1994. In 1995, movement of interest rates resembled that of 1993 with the 10-year Treasury yield plunging again from a cyclical high of 8% to 5.7%. During the first six months of 1996, the 10-year Treasury yield rose again by more than 100 basis points to 6.9%. This wide swing in interest rates was caused by the Fed initially tightening credit to contain the threat of inflation due to robust economic growth. Later on, however, the Fed eased credit to save the economy from slipping into recession. The gyration of interest rates significantly heightened volatility. During this four-year period, it was not unusual to witness volatility topping 20%, a level that rarely existed in the 1980s. More significant, volatile interest rates sent prepayments soaring and plunging. Issuance of REMICs reached record levels in the beginning of the period but collapsed in early 1994. By contrast, housing activity during this period staged one of the most impressive recoveries from the near-recession levels of the previous period. Also, FRMs remained the predominant form of mortgage finance during most of this period. All of these factors pressured the benchmark yield spread to widen.

Index